TAO I CHING

The Mystic Gateway

TAO I CHING

The Mystic Gateway

Tom Leworthy

Cover picture
edited detail of "First Entrance Gate to the Temple of Confucius, Ching-hai"
Thomas Allom 1842

TOM LEWORTHY © 2008
Published by Illustrious Artworks
ISBN 978-0-9557363-0-8

TAO I CHING

Contents

TAO I CHING

Introduction

There is a lot more going on than you are aware of, in front of you, and around you, all the time. There is a dynamic flow of energy running through the world that takes you, and everything, with it.

TAO is the great flow of energy running through the universe. This flow alternates between two different directions. One towards material involvement and control, and the other towards spiritual awareness and contentment. Your life may be taken-up with all sorts of responsibilities, involvements, and enjoyments, and the world is full enough to provide you with everything you need. While this takes-up most of your time, you may not be aware that the world is also full of other qualities of light, space, sound, movement and energy, that introduce you to another reality.

It is through Mystic Gateways that you enter the everyday world with a different approach and perception of the present moment. The most obvious and greatest of these Mystic Gateways is The TAO I CHING.

The TAO I CHING will provide you with advice, guidance, and direction in the world, and a way to use your personal energy that is both effective and easy. The flow of your own energy is revealed, and changed, through the use of the HEXAGRAM symbols of The TAO I CHING. These HEXAGRAM symbols were originally written down in ancient China some 3000 years ago as part of The I Ching, 'The Book of Change'. Simply by using these symbols in your everyday life, as a source of information and insight, you have the way to inner peace, fulfilment, and happiness, in this busy modern world of ours.

Recognising TAO, and being able to modify the flow of energy through yourself and your life, changes everything. The TAO I CHING will show you how to live in the present, more effectively, with inner peace and confidence.

TAO I CHING

TAO

The Immensity Of The Universe

Three or four thousand years ago in Ancient China someone came up with the idea of TAO, as the source, and functioning, of all things. TAO was so vast it was beyond definition, but the effects could be seen everywhere. Because of its' universal and spiritual perspective, further attempts to classify TAO, and to encapsulate it within a man-made system, were discouraged. The mystery of the universe did not lend itself readily to definition.

"TAO named, is not TAO"

The presence of TAO is all pervading and ever-present in Man and in the Natural World around us, but the only way to explain it was to resort to contradiction.

"Look, it can't be seen
Listen, you can't hear it
Learn, there is no way
TAO is nowhere to be found
yet it supports all things."

"Tao Te Ching" Lao Tzu

Attempts to get closer to the way TAO works, again, meets with a similar response.

"TAO never acts and yet is never inactive."

Your personal reactions to all of this can also lead to problems and more contradictions.

> "By intending you deviate. TAO belongs neither
> to knowing or not knowing. Knowing is false
> understanding; not knowing is blind ignorance.
> If you really understand TAO beyond doubt,
> it is like the empty sky."
>
> Nan-ch'uan

PHOTOGRAPHIC EVIDENCE

Symbolically, TAO could look like this

TAO contains nothing, and yet exists (see the shadow).
It is access, but there is no direction.
It is without time.   It is a gateway.
It is Nothing.   It can be filled with any image.

TAO is an idea, albeit a very spiritual and metaphysical one, used to express our wonder and involvement in the universe. In the Twentyfirst Century not only can TAO be defined, but its' effects and operation can be plainly seen in yourself, and in your everyday world.

TAO is a state, condition, or energy interplay, in a material, physical, and spiritual sense. It is *the underlying structure and functioning of the universe* and exists *as an influence in the world*. TAO has no rational or intellectual, or even spiritual, justification. *It is just within each different momentary situation you find yourself in.* TAO works without purpose, and in all circumstances, good and bad. It is 'impersonal' (and this is how it is recognised) and is often seen as chance and change.

Your life, and your reality, is not a fixed point in space and time but a reflection of your present awareness, and your thoughts, and memories. Your social and material situation possesses no energy apart from what you, and others, put in to it, and TAO can be seen *as a reflection of your energy in the world.*

Energy is your connection with the world and to the universe. TAO is also the unseen power of energy flowing through the world, and its' effects can be witnessed by you in the movements and changes in your physical, material, and social life. **TAO is the great flow of energy that runs through the universe.** This is the movement of chance and change, sometimes known as 'The Way'. You could follow TAO as a sort of path through life by understanding or appreciating the 'laws of energy', or simply be moved by the flow.

Your world changes as you change, and as you go through life. Energy moves and changes everything. Strange things happen. Anything can happen. Your daily life can be magical and something more than just 'materialistic'. It is essential that you no longer think of TAO as a mystery, an alternative idea, or spiritual luxury, for it is the way you use this energy that determines how successful and happy you are in life. An awareness and understanding of TAO is not just for monks on a spiritual journey, but for all of us, whatever walk of life.

This flow of energy empowers all things.
"Actively doing nothing"

"Going with the flow"

THE FLOW OF ENERGY

A Whole New Perspective

This peaceful scene is made up of countless millions
of electrons each giving off boundless energy.

A great energy flow exists in the universe. This flow of energy is an influence, not a force, even though it is sometimes called "The Life Force". It is a vitality or movement *that can be influenced or re-directed at any time*. There are two aspects of this energy (or types, for ease of understanding) which form a balance between Man and Nature (environment), between Man and Man (social), and between Nature and Nature (Earth and sky, in the elemental).

**You participate in this flow of energy
through your attitude and awareness in life**,
through

Inflowing Energy　　　OR　　　**Outflowing Energy**

▬▬▬▬▬　　　　　　　▬▬　▬▬

These two energies, correspond directly to the construction of the symbols in The TAO I CHING

You can, and will, get caught–up in these flows that take you to 'predetermined' ends or consequences. Knowing where, and why, these flows operate, and their respective merits and drawbacks, puts you in a position to navigate a way through life. The influence of these flows of energy extends to all areas of your life, from the physical and material, to the emotional, mental, and spiritual. This energy flow determines the course and quality of your life.

Inflowing Energy

Inflowing Energy *is used to produce an end result, and to increase or exercise power.* This is based upon your past experiences and future hopes, the use of logic and reason, your beliefs, standards, values, motivation, and codes of conduct. **It is energy used in mental and physical avenues to achieve a goal, seek a reward, or activate a plan**. Inflowing Energy is the dynamic, competitive, and assertive, energy that drives the material world. Inflowing Energy is basically *calculating, to gain, to assume, to defend.*

Inflowing Energy exists in your desire for power and control, and is reinforced by intellectual reasoning, the logic of cause and effect, and all your notions of significance and meaning. It's about determination, and is often forceful. This energy flow can be channelled through passion, emotion, strong discipline, and conditioned thinking. This 'type' of energy, or flow of energy, is normally found in people and animals. Social ambition and hunting are examples of this 'single minded' energy.

Outflowing Enegy

Outflowing Energy *is used to exercise proficiency or pleasure, and implemented now in the present.* With Outflowing Energy you adapt, demonstrate, or observe, under all conditions, modifying everything you have contact with. **It is energy used in mental and physical avenues to express, or enjoy, an experience, for its own sake**. Outflowing Energy is the expressive, expanding and creative, energy that influences everything. Outflowing Energy is basically *expressive, to produce, to enjoy, to use.*

Outflowing Energy is an expression or state of being, sometimes an appreciation or delight, and is often spontaneous or creative. This 'type', or flow, of energy is normally found in the Natural Environment, in people, and occasionally in animals. The weather, laughter, and sunbathing, are examples of this 'influencing' energy.

The Flow of Energy in Man

Inflowing Energy		Outflowing Energy	
EXPERIENCE	SIGNIFICANCE	OBSERVATION	TRUST
MEANING	PURPOSE	ACCEPTANCE	USE
EXPECTATION	MOTIVATION	ENTHUSIASM	ENJOYMENT
LOGIC	REASON	INTUITION	SPONTANEITY
CONTROL	REACTION	CREATIVE	EXPRESSION
"materialistic"		"spiritual"	
TIME RELATED		IN THE PRESENT only	

You'll find Outflowing Energy in the pleasure of doing something by naturally expressing yourself through art, or music, for instance, in a hobby, leisure activities, or in something that you are good at, or in the enjoyment of sport. 'Playing to win', however, introduces competition and Inflowing Energy, so that both 'types' of energy could be found in the same activity. You may not be aware of it, or think it important, but only one desire or drive (and flow of energy) can exist at one time, and whether or not you enjoy yourself *and* compete, the energy can only flow in one direction at a time. **One directional flow of energy will predominate**. Your desires and intentions, and your attitude and awareness, follow, or determine, your energy output, *in a flow of energy that is automatic.* Your mind and body, like trees and water, act like a conducting rod or link for this flow of energy.

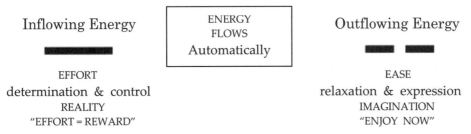

Inflowing Energy	ENERGY FLOWS Automatically	Outflowing Energy
EFFORT		EASE
determination & control		relaxation & expression
REALITY		IMAGINATION
"EFFORT = REWARD"		"ENJOY NOW"

The flow of energy is directed, as it is naturally with most people, through (Left) 'BRAIN CENTRED' activity, to control or make things, or to acquire, and use. You'll use Inflowing Energy in your work, your home, and to achieve your ambitions. To direct your energies through 'HEART CENTRED' activity, by using feelings and responses, requires a different approach. This is similar to the (Right) brain functions associated with intuition, insight, and creativity, which are usually only used when you need to express another view of reality, or when you relax or adjust your views. It's the different sensibility, sensitivity, and awareness, that comes from Outflowing Energy that allows you to be more at ease with yourself and the world.

Inflowing Energy	Outflowing Energy
▬▬▬▬▬▬▬	▬▬ ▬▬
The rough and tumble of THE WORLD "A piece of the action"	The inner quiet of THE HEART "Peace of mind"
You must have the determination to succeed, and apply discipline and control, to achieve results	The world will provide you with everything you need through chance and change, if you let it
TO CONSTRUCT	TO PLAY
▬▬▬▬▬▬▬	▬▬ ▬▬
with commitment through time and effort	with the free and spontaneous use of the materials at hand
TO CONTROL	TO ENJOY

In a busy world, as in an active mind, there is no room for peace and quiet, for there is just too much to do. Effort and worry, plans and control (Inflowing Energy) are admirably suited to this hectic life of involvement and identification, but little else. By 'switching off' the mental directives of reaction and control, and by accepting the situation for what it is (and it does change whatever you do), you can live in this world with composure and peace of mind (Outflowing Energy). The outward flow of energy is of course blocked by the use of that same energy in an inflowing manner through more involvement, competition, and conflict.

Inflowing Energy *has most of the action and apparent control.* Your striving and determination, and the struggle of Inflowing Energy, appears strengthening and offers you the prospect of future benefits. This dynamic energy flow can certainly give you the impression of identity, vitality, and 'getting things done', but it comes at a cost. *The energy required to do something for an end result requires constant renewal,* otherwise it becomes used-up. This can be seen in the effort of exercise, the stress of work, and in the aging process. To 'get anywhere' or to progress, you'll need to do more of the same, or increase your effort or concentration. It is when people get older that the price of Inflowing Energy becomes more apparent, with a constant struggle to 'keep up' with the world. This can happen at any time of life, and at some point people give-up, or are exhausted, or are overtaken by events. By being more open to the wonder and possibilities of the world and the present moment, at whatever age, you will actually maintain your energy level in awareness and contentment.

Outflowing Energy *offers satisfaction, ease, and acceptance.* The energy you use in 'expressive' activities increases energy output, and it all takes place in the present moment. The more fun you get, and the more enthusiastic you are, the easier it is to overcome any problem, and the further you'll go. Creativity knows no bounds, enjoyment is shared, and laughter can be contagious, even if you don't know the joke.

There is an 'automatic' flow of energy which takes you, and others, and all things, to 'predetermined' ends, and while some consequences appear more attractive, there is a price to pay. The 'price' will be paid by your energy consumption and output. With involved control, competition, opposition, and conflict, you consume energy. By doing what is easy, through enjoyment and relaxation, you accumulate energy.

Inflowing Energy is not to be misunderstood. It has progressive organising tendencies, but little capacity for sustained satisfaction. It comes from the power to do things, and the desire for control. Power is the expression of your Will, directly or indirectly, over others or yourself. Inflowing Energy acts on itself, for itself. Outflowing Energy is not to be underestimated. The change brought about by even the smallest relaxation of effort can alter the whole situation. Outflowing Energy comes from the pleasure of your situation, directly or indirectly, through the world of people, places, sensations, and things. Outflowing Energy acts now, in the present, regardless.

> In ANY course of action you WILL select
> either Inflowing Energy or Outflowing Energy,
> and 'the flow' will take you down either route.

THE ENERGY OF THE WORLD

Grow Rich

Inflowing Energy *is the drive towards achievement.* It is for getting things done through motivation, hard work, discipline, and control. It is realistic in that it answers your experience and expectations in life. It will give you purpose and meaning, and a sense of vitality from knowing who you are, and how right you are. If you think in terms of ambition and effort, plans and controls, your past and your future, you are using Inflowing Energy.

In the very busy world of social and family life, of education, work, and personal advancement, there is a demand and desire for results and rewards. Inflowing Energy is your hold on the world. That hold on reality is maintained by the tight grip of commitment, responsibility, standards and values, continuous involvement, and the prospect of power and pleasure. Welcome to the real world of hard work and play. By working hard you could afford that holiday of a lifetime. You could build a better future for yourself and your childrens' children. You might find a name for yourself through your job, your talents, or your family. You might just seek a better standard of living, entertainment, or a purpose in life. These choices, these directions, are the expression of Inflowing energy.

Inflowing Energy *represents the struggle, striving, achievement, success or failure : the spirit of determination.* This imparts that feeling of being alive, of doing something, or being someone. Even if you don't measure-up, or if there are any material obstacles, delays, or dissatisfactions, you will still be fully occupied as you deal with these. Such is 'the way of the world' that you will willingly, or unconsciously, adopt Inflowing Energy in order to get the material and emotional satisfaction you want out of life. However, there will rarely be any relaxation of effort (except for that annual holiday), for there will always be an element of dissatisfaction, or the desire for more, whatever your status in life.

Those that use Inflowing Energy (and you can recognise them) will be in a state of constant reaction or control in the world, and in themselves. This state of affairs need not imply permanent conflict. On the contrary, it is through this 'opposition' and involvement, and the demand for results, that gives you a sense of purpose and direction. Your strength and position in the world is balanced by conflicting and opposing forces, in others, and unforeseen events. This flow of energy will divert your attention so that *all your vitality is expressed in maintaining the status quo, or working towards some future ambition or later reward.* This impression of progress dominates most people's lives. In this way, Inflowing Energy takes-up the whole of your attention and uses the world as place for obtaining satisfaction through others, or within yourself. All of this seems not only natural and effective, but unavoidable. Your situation, and continued existence, will continually demand this type, or flow, of energy.

When you use Inflowing Energy your thoughts become enclosed within a 'personalised framework', single-minded ambition, approach, or 'your way of doing things'. Your notion of time, and the importance you place on it, is a function of Inflowing Energy. You'll see time as a commodity to be used, and your life as a means to more, or in the fear of loss, as an incentive, reaction, or reason, for involved concern. This energy is inward directed to gain and to hold, and is supported by all your stored thoughts and feelings. Inflowing Energy will present all the methods, and the reasons, to keep you on a time line that has already started. That's how urgent and serious it is !

Most of your thinking processes and experiences are orientated towards an active involvement in issues of time. Your concern over the daily rush, your present age, and the thousand other time related issues, is the biggest pull of Inflowing Energy. If you are unaware of all of this, there will be an automatic exchange of energy depending on your situation. Such automatic exchanges revolve around actions and reactions, desire and gratification, effort and struggle.

Seven Ways to recognise people who use Inflowing Energy

1. Very busy, or very tired, sometimes both. Always active. Being tired is an active flow of, and does require a lot of, Inflowing Energy. Time, deadlines, and achievement, are central factors.

2. Such people are often 'full of themselves', their ambitions and intentions. They have plenty of advice, justification, and reasons.

3. Status, or lack of it, is a major concern.

4. Commitment and competition are seen as a measure of credibility. Involved in many different spheres of life, in the practical, financial, and social, issues of career and family, or political, religious, or intellectual pursuits.

5. Strong or fixed beliefs. Holding on to one view. Control must be exercised, or sought as a guiding force, or followed through a set of rules, laws, standards, or conditions.

6. Noise, much talking, and strong reactions. The display of emotion and physical demonstration. Violence.

7. Quick to make comparisons and judgements. Insistent, controlling, or aggressive. Negativity. Pessimism and criticism. Saying "NO" with great conviction, or disgust.

This flow of energy, these involved concerns and thoughts, cannot be resolved or achieved immediately, so more attention and effort is required to maintain your position. You are in this world full of things, status, responsibilities and distractions, and your mind will keep on supplying you with new ways, hopes, fears, and reasons, to involve you, one way or another. Your place is determined by your mind and body, socially, and physically – who you are. This, however, is over-ruled by your thoughts, intentions and determination, and personality, and the use of your talents, circumstances, desires and reactions. This is a seemingly endless process of achievement or adjustment.

There is no final position of status or authority unless it is supported by Inflowing Energy, because everything is moving and changing. The time to achieve your plans, the money to realise your ambitions, and the stamina for all of this, requires Inflowing Energy. You will not finally sort-out, solve, or answer, this world of complexity, diversity, variety, beauty, chance and change. If you do, the price you pay is in the amount of energy required to sustain your position. Of course, there will always be the promise of eventual success, or satisfaction, or being saved, or winning the lottery, *at some future date*. There may even be that fear of death, disease, or loss of control, but in the meantime there are more immediate concerns about your survival, the direction you are going in, your day to day concerns, and the possibility of even greater rewards.

There is, however, something else on offer.

THE LIGHT OF THE WORLD

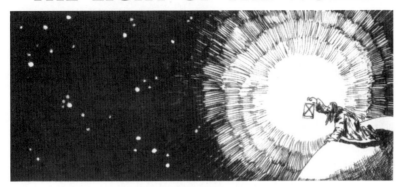

Our Man In The Shadows

Outflowing Energy *is effortless, and is in the pleasure of doing something now*, not later or for some future reward. It is outgoing, immediate, and often spontaneous. You can see this mostly when you're engaged in 'leisure activities', in moments of peace and quiet, relaxing, meditation, or perhaps when you're on holiday – all of which are 'out' of 'normal life'. Outflowing Energy *presents an attitude of acceptance, of fun, enthusiasm and optimism, and sometimes a spiritual outlook.*

Instead of confronting the world, and being continually organised by timetables, circumstances, and people, just stop what you are doing long enough to look around you, and listen. It's what you do when you're on holiday. Withdraw your reactions and demands, enjoy what is around you, and let others 'do their worst, or their best'. It will give you a fresh new outlook. The world won't become more spiritual or easier, you will ! As in all your activities and enjoyments, the truth is, no one else, no conditions, or any amount of money, can do this for you. Regardless of what you think and do, the world runs to its' own time and agenda through the great forces of chance and change (TAO).

Chance and change are automatic. *You are already in a system that runs itself.* Problems, decisions, frustrations, and emotional events will continue to turn-up with regularity. If you do not over-react with Inflowing Energy and all that concern and effort, you'll see that the world will provide a solution or 'way out' every time, and this is encouraged by your relaxed confidence.

Usually, when anything happens, you 'take it in' and take it seriously, or emotionally. This is Inflowing Energy, with all its' later reactions and reinforcements. Next time, 'just look', without any personal thoughts, and let

17

things happen. You are still involved – you cannot stop that – but the emptier or quieter you are, the fuller you become of a new kind of energy and awareness. We all have dreams, ambitions, or goals, but once you are clear about them, and you've made your plans, let your thoughts and concerns about how, when, and where, go. That's all you have to do is to attend to the details of each day, as they are presented to you, and you can even use the HEXAGRAMS to guide you in the right direction.

Outflowing Energy is automatic. You accept it, and it flows through you naturally. The present moment exists merely for this to happen, to give you space, opportunities, and time. The secret is to look out all the time, and listen. Try it ! This is not a passive waiting, but *an active flow of energy that increases* your awareness and prospects. This 'casual' listening will give you a greater sense of the actual place and time around you. When you concentrate on your own objectives to the exclusion of everything else, you miss a very strange fact. Every room, and space, and every moment, is important in its own right, not just as a means to an end, but as a conduit for energy. Events, opportunities, and choices, are presented to you all the time. The world is structured, and operates, to provide opportunities, and Outflowing Energy *will bend all the material rules of possibility and time*, through chance and change *to answer your needs. All of this is provided* in the situations and circumstances that you face everyday and every week. You can only see this in the present moment as it presents itself to you. The world is gratuitous, and large enough to offer you all these chances, and impersonal, in that it operates regardless of who you are, what you know, care, or think.

Outflowing Energy only flows through the present moment. That present moment may seem elusive or insubstantial, but it opens-up a whole new way of looking at the world. The old 'automatic' way of regarding the present as a consequence of the past, or as a means to the future, or as the dull backdrop to your life, is obsolete, and can only be promoted or sustained through the use of more Inflowing Energy, in your own reaction, regret, desire and gratification. Outflowing Energy is more direct, and a lot simpler, than you thought. You can add light into your life and the world, now, today, very easily. You only have to smile, or go for a walk, say a positive word (to yourself, or others), encourage someone, 'take five minutes off' whatever you are doing, or tidy-up your immediate surroundings. Act on what you can see, and what is closest to you *now*, whatever your job or position might be, and do it *with ease*.

16 Ways of Outflowing Energy

1. Shine all reflective surfaces in your immediate surroundings. Shine-up chrome, metal, plastic, and glass. Add some light into the material world. The next time you look, you'll feel the difference. Look–out for 'sparkly light' in the natural environment.
    You "shine out !" – *just smile.* You don't need a reason.

2. Stop thinking, just for a moment. Let go of all those thoughts about the thousand and one things you should, or could, do. For a moment let go of all those memories, hopes, justifications, day dreams, dissatisfactions, comparisons and speculations. In that quiet moment you recharge your batteries. When you do this it may seem odd or empty, or perhaps pointless, so, instead, fill the space with what is actually around you now. Just listen, and look.

3. Be "OPEN", and watch the effect. **O**ptimism **P**romotes **E**nthusiasm **N**ow. Treat the day as an adventure, or exploration, into undiscovered territory. Notice everything from the climate to the strangeness of the environment, and the inhabitants. Allow TAO to change your route, to challenge you, or surprise you, and show you wonders. Let chance and change provide the variety and diversity.

4. Just say "This *is* easy" when you do anything, regardless of the circumstances, or whether or not you think it makes any difference. Remarkably, it changes everything. By adding positive and encouraging words into every situation you can totally transform your world. How strange, that what we say 'is'.

5. "HELP" others through **H**umour, **E**ncouragement, **L**isten, and **P**ropose, but do *not* give advice.

6. Take a walk around where you live. Look at it as a space, rather than a place. This space extends in all directions. The weather and time of day are a part of that space.

7. Tread quietly through the world. This will do wonders for your heart.

8. Never react. You can't stop Inflowing Energy, so, divert it, distract it, or ignore it. Regardless of the situation, do not use negative words or comments. (You can think what you like).

9. Use just a little less energy in your responses. Only you create the internal tension, so let the world go for once (it won't make any difference). That reaction, opinion, attitude, or viewpoint, you have may actually stop you seeing the world as it is. You don't have to like it, or make any judgement or comment. Just listen and observe, and it will make a big difference. It's a lot easier than you've allowed for.

10. "Make light of it all". Never give material concerns any more time or attention than necessary – just deal with them. Use humour, and ease, to make it seem as if you don't take it all *quite so seriously*. Be able to laugh at yourself.

11. Each day give someone, a pet, plant, or any living thing, your total undivided attention for just five minutes. What you give-out your heart receives later, in abundance.

12. Allow the world to talk to you, through people, situations, and events. Spend a few minutes looking out of that window you always pass. Every window reveals something, if you give it time. Even trees and rooms will talk to you, if you let them.

13. Observe TAO. Look at the world around you as though it 'just exists' without reasons, meaning, direction, or cosmic purpose. Try it, and you'll find that with all of that removed, you are just left with *"It's amazing !*

14. Mind your own business (only). Let others, and the rest of the of the world, get on with it. The world doesn't need your reaction.

15. Enjoy yourself ! Only you can make yourself comfortable, wherever you are. Avoid logical assumptions, conventional methods, or traditional arguments, if they delay, or deny you, your comfort and happiness. Don't take second best, or be tempted by future offers.

16. Let go of your past. It is the present that supports you.

You cannot hold on to TAO. You cannot store it up, or depend on it for power or control. This is *not* about being better organised, more sure of yourself, or changing your attitudes or approach. No matter how hard you try, you will not change in that way, for in the trying you simply *divert that same energy elsewhere*. Your mind will continue to present some interesting options through your experience, beliefs, and sense of justice and truth. The rightness of your own assumptions and attitudes about the world and your place in The Great Scheme of Things, and all your thoughts, *will* keep you diverted. If you question you will get reasoned and justified answers to keep you using Inflowing Energy.

There is only one response to this dilemma, and that is in the Chinese term *"mu"*, which is often translated as a negative, but is, in the true Taoist tradition, *I don't know. Does it matter ?* No answer is required here. This will sound irresponsible because the world, with all its' events and enticements, is constructed for this very reason – to keep you questioning, and involved.

There is an easier way to achieve your goals in life, and be happy and stress free. It is through an inner change of energy or direction. The opposite of all the involvement and control is 'letting go', but not to take-up something else. The opposite of tension is not relaxation, as some sort of method or practice, but 'letting go'. You only have to 'let things be', to let Outflowing Energy flow. That is, you let go of that personal (inner) determination to control people, and situations, and let (outer) chance and change happen – as it will, whatever you do.

The dramatic and obvious fact is that chance and change rule the world, and it affects us all. It is this fact that Inflowing Energy challenges, endlessly. The way of the world, the status quo, and the involvement of *Inflowing Energy, can only reflect or repeat itself.* It cannot cause change, only a repetition, and from this there is no escape.

It is THOUGHT that connects you to the notion that you must always take control, but this is merely the expression of Inflowing Energy, through some very demanding or desiring thoughts. If you control, practice, or try, you are inadvertently, or consciously, using Inflowing Energy. With such powerful forces in play, the notion of 'letting go' will not appeal, or even appear effective. So, here you are again, in a world out of your control, and ruled by chance and change. All your use of Inflowing Energy serves only to involve you further in your own reactions, and yet, surprisingly, there is an alternative. *That alternative exists in the same world, but is empowered by a different energy.*

21

The present moment consumes everything – chance, change, control, you and your thoughts, and actions. You are connected to the present moment only through Outflowing Energy. This works automatically, and the results are a little surprising, and far-reaching. Just let TAO and the present moment do all the work. What is called 'spontaneous action' (action without being dictated by thought) is probably the closest the Western mind can get to the Taoist term "*wu wei*", which means 'without effort' or 'effortless action'. Thought may well be present, but it's in the background. Effort may well be present, but it's not the controlling force. By employing one or more of those 16 Ways you not only change your own energy flow, but that of the world. If you follow any of those Ways on a daily basis you will notice a difference in your well-being in a week, through that extra energy you've created. You can transform yourself and the world by the smallest of actions. In some strange way it is the smallest actions, that happen now, that produce the greatest results. This is not generally appreciated, or understood, because your attention is taken away from the present, to produce more plans, and control. According to this view, the present is already out of date, in the rush to the future. Time and action are bound together as a process of control.

When you actually see TAO in action it causes an extra, perhaps unexpected, response – a smile. When you see the simplicity and 'speed' of it all, you can smile at fate, and your own previous rushing about, and all your efforts to control events, people, and time. The first thing you'll notice is that things seem to slow down a bit. You'll also notice, when you are not preoccupied, that there is actually a lot going on that is both subtle and calming. Your *awareness is the only thing that can create more out of this world*.

The world right now, around you, wherever you are, is absolutely full of Outflowing Energy. This flow of Outflowing Energy is released when you do not block it with your thoughts. Look, and be, in *the present moment*, and you'll realise how much time you've been spending in the past, in the future, and 'in your head'. Stop going-in to your thoughts. Your thoughts will continue to naturally arise when needed, and you can still apply them to solve those problems that need organisation or attention.

Seven Ways to recognise people who use Outflowing Energy

1. 'Unworldly', or 'child like', or seen as naïve. There is no obvious show of status. There is the expression of openness, and a relaxed confidence and directness.

2. A sense of calm or inner peace. At ease with the world, themselves, and their environment. Quiet disposition and lifestyle, and comfortable in themselves.

3. Detached. No firm allegiances to family or society. Non-judgemental, and accepting, but can see people and situations for what they are.

4. Apparently motiveless. Little, or no, competitive spirit. Apparent 'unused' talent. There is an inner certainty that leads to a dynamic drive and energy.

5. They enjoy the simple pleasures of life. An appreciation of the weather and the 'ordinary'. They will cross all boundaries of taste, society, and culture. They have a natural understanding of who they are, and are not fooled by status, self-importance, or ego.

6. Open to many views, but not committed to any. Not inclined to react. Clarity, or openness of mind. A simple ability to listen without offence, or opinion.

7. Light hearted, optimistic, generous, and a sense of humour. Enjoy saying "YES", sometimes unexpectedly, or spontaneously.

Released into the world, you'll find it's not the place you thought it was. The natural world, the weather, the environment, and the situations you are in, and the people around you, all provide you with opportunities, interest, support, and a place to be. Outflowing Energy is a way through the world, that lets the world come to you in all its' variety and abundance. That's all you have to do is *"Take it – easy"*. Find what interests, amuses, or challenges, you. Wherever you are, look for light, comfort, and companionship. Spend time now, in the present, as if it's all you had.

IT'S NOT ALL ACTION.
YOU GET LOTS OF TIME OFF,
AND GOOD COMPANY
TO SHARE IT WITH.

PLENTY OF TIME OFF

When you step out of the 'thought provoking equation' you will make the remarkable discovery that TAO moves on its own, and pretty slowly, and you have plenty of time to consider your response, to act, and to take time off. It also offers you something else. There is a lot more going on around you right now in sound, light, and movement. Just stop what you are reading now, and listen and look, for just two minutes. The world is talking to you, and it's a pretty interesting place even before anything happens. When you get the equation right you enter a world that is spontaneous and full. It's time to enjoy life, to step away from the seeking, stress, and control, and be open to the chance and change that will improve your life.

At first, this way of 'trusting' chance and change may seem irresponsible, or even daunting, but through your 'spontaneous' selection of HEXAGRAMS you will find a Way presented to you. You'll let go of the idea that you could actually control anything, and find an easier way through life.

It's called 'living in the present'.

LIVING IN THE PRESENT

From Here, To Eternity

We use the notion of time to put some order and organisation into our lives. Historical events, industry and science, as well as personal development, can all be conveniently allocated a certain time or age, and this introduces the notion of progress towards achievement, maturity, or perfection. Each phase and activity reaches towards, or serves, an end result. Time, far from being just a period, or collection of moments, has necessarily become a sort of organisational framework for the measurement of progress, of work, travel, history, and family. This measurement of time is fixed and overlaid onto almost every activity, to provide a framework for social order, to facilitate planning, calculate profit, to record events, and estimate speed and distance.

Beyond all this organisation, if you wanted to see what time was really like, you would either have to take some 'mind altering' drugs, or use your imagination by way of explanation. Imagine holding a pack of cards in one hand and slowly flicking through the top edge of the entire pack with the other hand. Each card, momentarily exposed, represents the present moment, rapidly followed by the next (after a second), and so on. At each moment you are momentarily exposed to the world, or made aware. For a moment there is self awareness, but very little time to think or act. Planned actions could overlap from one moment to the next, but only if you could maintain a chain of thought. *You have about 5 seconds to 2 minutes in each moment, where your awareness is continuous and uninterrupted. You live momentarily,* and if you thought about it this could be a little frightening, and, perhaps, best ignored. This is the basic operation of time, but your perception of it, and use of it, must be modified in order to achieve certain things. If you place less attention on the momentary experiences, you can think in longer terms by establishing thought patterns that are already complete. You can leave the moments look after themselves while you work towards your objective. *The completeness of the thought or motivation is a factor that is fundamental to your use of time.*

In other cultures, this organisation of time takes on a different perspective from the Western preoccupation with industry and progress. Perhaps, an Indian notion of time might resemble a river that flows through the land. A person caught in the current would experience a duration of involvement or movement through this land (life), but be dependant on the current (of events). The river may flood or contract in season, leading to the notion of full or lean times. From a small start, the river ultimately, and predictably, flows into the sea. Time here represents a fluid state, but set on a course. It is something we are in, and must adapt to, and not something we use for our convenience.

The Chinese might also use a natural element to describe the influence of time when they compare it to the wind. The wind blows across the landscape, moving small things, bending trees, or providing a cooling breeze. The wind might bring rain, or itself become part of a raging storm. Here, time acts as a framework for the expression of either divine of human activity. When the wind is becalmed we have quiet times, and when there are gale force winds we have upheaval and physical changes. Time is seen as a changing vehicle for the forces we might, or might not, be able to control.

Apart from these two metaphors, of the river and the wind, and your imaginary pack of cards, there is another notion of time. Phrases like "time flew by", or "the time wasn't right", and in response to some emergencies, "time went into slow motion", point to something else. Here your involvement, intuition, or instinct, play a part, and time becomes a contracting or expanding experience. It may seem odd that you can experience and understand time in different ways, but this is merely a reflection of your perception and mental capacity. With your imaginary pack of cards you could also lay out the whole pack, and arrange them into sets, or number them consecutively, to show that events are related, or that there is a progressive, or at least ordered, development. You live in a seemingly eternal present. On reflection you may, and do, connect moments into meaningful periods.

If one thing remains constant it is "the ebb and flow of life", "life's ups and downs", or movements in world events or personal fortunes. This brings us to the discovery that the ancient Chinese made, that change occurs, not as a consequence of 'time', but by virtue of a shift, or difference, in energy. In other words, *the process of change* has little to do with time, control, or progress, and may indeed look like chance.

Change may manifest in situations and circumstances beyond your control, or be the result of intended action. All of these changes take place in time, or to be more precise, it is by the observation of change that you become aware of the notion of time. It would be the Western mind that saw a continual development in such affairs, and to determine that cause and effect were the forces at play. The Eastern mind might see scientific and social progress, but contend that other heavenly forces, or fate, play a great part.

According to the Taoists, two complimentary aspects of energy make up the whole of existence. 'YIN' is dark, negative, weak and passive, and 'YANG' is light, positive, strong and active. The female/male attributes also applied to these aspects are a crude approximation of receptive and expressive forces. These two principles interact to produce all substances and objects. Each item, person, and even situation, is therefore possessed of YIN or YANG qualities. Despite the predilection of the Chinese to list every single thing and ascribe to it YIN/YANG qualities, it should not be taken too literally since there is only one 'substance' in the universe (T'ai Chi = supreme energy, the absolute), which has two aspects. Change is the meeting (joining or conflict) of two aspects of the same basic substance. The basic substance in Man, the world, and in the universe, which is subject to change, is energy. You cannot see this substance or energy, but you can directly observe the effects of the interaction between its' two aspects as change. Fundamental to Taoist thought is this constant change, flux, or dynamic interaction between YIN and YANG. Perhaps the simplest analogy is to view T'ai Chi as the universe and everything, and TAO as the way it functions, or, more precisely, the functioning of it. Inflowing Energy and Outflowing Energy express this movement of energy.

> *"Life's problems, involvements, triumphs, and concerns,*
> *are but a shadow play of energy."*

On a very personal level Inflowing Energy will make itself felt through your thoughts, and particularly on those thoughts and actions related to time. You introduce 'time' to add direction , or tension, 'to get things done'. If you could

27

remove most of your concerns about time (the deadlines, 'living for the weekend', 'not enough time', 'time lost', your age, and the unresolved future), you would actually see your situation *as it is in the present*. The next time you have the urge to 'use', or worry over, time, step back *for a moment* and 'let go'. Let go of your control and thoughts on the consequences, and you will find that the world will just continue, as it always has done, without you.

The world functions with or without you. The world will continue as before, but in that moment *you can stay in the present*, and choose to act, or not. When you stop your thoughts, reaction, or worried involvement, you will see another layer of activity (TAO). Now, most strange of all, is the fact that time is grounded in place, or your awareness of the place that you find yourself in at any moment, *not* thought. 'Here' and 'now' are intimately linked and may be seen as the same 'thing'.

It is only in the present moment that energy moves. You need to be aware of the moment. To 'overcome' your incessant thoughts you only need to be aware of your own responses to one thing after another. Just watch yourself. This is a basic, and very personal, awareness of how you are going about things during the day. It is when you embrace 'the everyday', and leave the limitations, injustices, and faults, go, that you can improve and go forward. The odd and amazing fact is that your personal opinion and reaction is not actually required, but most of the time you will forget, or get diverted, such is the pull of Inflowing Energy.

Living in the moment requires a different understanding of the automatic flow of energy. This flow of energy increases, develops, and expands, and in this flow of energy you can become more involved, or take it easy, and still live life to the full. It's not going to be like you think it is, and you won't loose any of your powers or personality. To be in the world without Inflowing Energy and your attitude and concerns may at first seem pointless, or at least unattractive, but it opens-up the world in a fuller, more dynamic, way, alert to every possibility, chance, and change.

Beyond the noise and pressure, there is another way which rests simply on unbiased observation with no thoughts, opinions, or attitude, otherwise you WILL condition, and impose your view on, everything you see. You only need to be open enough to accept what you see, whether you agree with it or not. When you let the world of involved reaction go, you can be at ease, spontaneous (if you want), clear sighted, effective, and always 'on time' – being here now.

TIME FOR INACTION

Each person's view of reality, and what is important in life, is, seemingly, different, and you may have noticed that, even between two or three people, there will be disagreement. Where three or more are gathered, when a committee is formed, there will be debate, dispute, conflict or compromise, because each has a different viewpoint. It is when each different faction or branch of politics, religion, or society, establishes a (single) view and the right to act and rule, that the problems arise. The basis of all the problems is not because of a difference in opinion or belief, but because of an attitude which uses an energy that is confrontational. The definition of attitude is 'a settled mode of thinking', indicating a set, or settled, behaviour. Even though this represents the status quo, it will *always react* to the conditions of the world.

Your ATTITUDE, and the way you think and act, requires a lot of energy to flow inwards to reinforce it, and strengthen it, to build up *an internal picture which is then applied in all circumstances*. This is a perpetually adjusting balance and, for most, Inflowing Energy is the 'default setting'. Your most natural response is to react, to seek confirmation, or *to question or deny any way other than your own*. Your attitude conditions the whole of your life, and to maintain this a lot of effort is required, and that means more Inflowing Energy.

You may have noticed the constant feeding that is required to sustain your interest, position, or lifestyle. The need and supply of Inflowing Energy can be delivered through any number of daily involvements and emotions, from personal gratifications, desires, and reactions to problems, your attention to social and world events, to watching TV. *.It is the mental fixation, desire, and emotional involvement, that keeps you going.* You'll never stop thinking and wanting, doing and gathering. When you strive, desire, or attempt to control, you use Inflowing Energy. You'll never arrive at perfection. You could make a profound, or secular, case for the journey itself, but the rules, reasons, and reactions, of religion, science, and society, will only involve you more. You will always be 'on the road' to somewhere, half way to getting something, or to 'being someone'. It would be like spending your whole life in an effort to amass enough money to finally retire and live in comfort and security, only to find that your happiness actually came from the struggle, the desire, anticipation, and control. The material world is constructed for, and thrives on, the continued use of Inflowing Energy through involvement and reaction, and your everyday thoughts and plans. In all of this you are helped by the Inflowing Energy that is in surplus in the world.

It is no coincidence that the material world is full of opposites and opposition, demanding a reaction, and that Inflowing Energy is so well suited to, and excels in, confrontation, control, and concern. Conflict is the central factor for it provides the reaction which further empowers this flow of energy. In a world of conflict and brutality, and of financial and material restrictions, it is obvious that Inflowing Energy rules the world (of Man), because people want more. To get it people use force, and the inequality in the world is sustained by confrontation, greed, and power. To oppose those who seek more control, power, status, and possessions, you will, apparently, have to apply similar tactics and strength.

FIGHT
FOR
PEACE

The rest of the world will tell you to get involved, get angry, react, do something ! As soon as you react or become involved, you too use this kind of energy. Whatever you do, the imperfect world remains. All worldly activity is the movement of energy. Nothing is complete, perfect, or static. It will always change, yet stay the same. Time consuming involvement diverts your energy through the prospect of greater control, over others and yourself, and the promise of satisfaction, power, or success. It becomes a way of life to work harder, to consume more, and to seek more diversions and control. When this approach takes over, deadlines cause stress, timetables regulate pleasure, and plans for the future encourage acquisition and anxiety. All this activity will take you away from an awareness of the present *as it is*, to replace it with a world as you see it, or want it. As you now see it, possibly, the present doesn't contain the 'perfection' you desire, or what you want, and to this end the future is more important to you. Inflowing Energy uses time 'as a means to an end'.

Beyond this, and more subtle still, is concern. This involves thinking for, and on behalf of, others, which at first seems entirely laudable, but it will distract you and use you to reflect the energy of the world. Be warned that there is also a pull to Inflowing Energy as an indulgence in negative thoughts, resentment, and disappointment, often seen as a dissatisfaction with others. This is something you can indulge in even though it is negative, for these emotions can seem quite delicious at times, or perhaps righteously justified. Your centre of attention and awareness is ever in danger of being reflected and channelled into an attitude of endless involvement in something that, in itself, will not change, but continually absorb energy. Inflowing Energy *does nothing but consume, and reflect your concern,* through continued involvement. Reaction fuels Inflowing Energy, and your attitude consumes energy. You will not prevail against Inflowing Energy without a fight, without reaction, and endless retaliation, **against an energy that thrives on such attention.**

It is not your circumstances that puts you in opposition to, or in competition with, the world, or makes you stressed or unhappy, but *self interest manifested in Inflowing Energy.* Self interest is not only legitimate but necessary, but it is almost always manifested in Inflowing Energy. To face the inevitable changes in life, the demands of work and family, society and relationships, with Inflowing Energy, is just asking for trouble !

This is what Inflowing Energy is constructed for, and does best.

Awkward as this may be to accept, when you see poverty, injustice, or violence, *your reaction*, indignation, fear or courage, is merely another expression of that same energy. If you follow your instincts it is likely that you will use Inflowing Energy, because it offers the prospects of control or power.

It is the reaction and confrontation that you have to avoid, even though you may be tempted or prompted by rightness or justice. Don't worry about others, and the state of the world, because it will always be like this, and it is endless. THE WORLD THRIVES ON INFLOWING ENERGY. Until you change your awareness you will not see this without a reaction. Your reaction doesn't actually help, but merely reinforces, or defines, the problem. This type of energy actually makes the world you live in unpleasant or unjust, demanding, and 'time pressured'.

There is another flow of energy available that is light and spontaneous, and 'easy going', through the expression of love, encouragement, and 'non-reaction'. Outflowing Energy is expressed through less effort in what is 'easy', as a natural expression (of who, or where, you are), and for no ulterior motive, reason, or expected reward. All of this will sound very odd, or impractical, because you believe you need to do things you don't want to, to achieve the ends you want. It's easier than that ! The worry and stress, conflict and control, is something you, and others, factor into the equation 'to get things done'. Things get done !, with or without you. For your own happiness and fulfilment in life there needs to be a natural flow of energy, without effort or control, otherwise you will NEVER give up the struggle.

When you see your position in this vast flow of energy, you'll realise that *awareness is the only thing you possess*. However, it is on this awareness, incomplete and unused, that you build (another layer of) attitude – your favourite collection of thoughts, responses, and behaviour – to cope, to be different, to be you, and to excel in the world. You actually change the direction of the energy passing through you. Inflowing Energy is 'automatic' in its' reaction and involvement, and, unless you 'slow down', you will miss just about everything that is actually going on around you. *It is your awareness that changes the world* NOT your concern, attitude, intentions, or control. Your awareness 'makes' reality, while your attitude merely reflects what you think onto the world. Without this awareness you will not change anything, but simply continue to *confront the world and consume energy as you have always done.*

Awareness contains all things. Call it 'consciousness', if you will. That awareness is open and creating more, or closed and 'feeding on itself'. What is consumed, or created, is ENERGY, which symbolically appears as a flow as it rushes to fill-up, empty, or move on. You can see this in The Four Dynamic Laws of Energy, which convert, increase, divert, and use up, energy.

The world is an arena, or playground, for the use and influence of Inflowing Energy and Outflowing Energy. The energy level in you, and in the world about you, exists in a dynamic balance, but is also in a state of constant change. It is in a state of change because *the influences of Inflowing Energy and Outflowing Energy increase or decrease your energy consumption and output.* You can spend as much energy thinking, worrying, and planning, as you do in physical work and social activity. All of this energy consumption is intimately connected to your level of awareness. The capacity for awareness is contained within you, or actually in the present moment. To go further, to increase your awareness, you need to look out, from an inner quiet, and listen. That awareness changes reality, and could introduce you to new worlds of perception.

The Mystic Gateway of the TAO I CHING introduces you to 64 HEXAGRAM symbols, each made up of six lines of energy. Each HEXAGRAM is a balance of energy based on shifting levels of consuming, constructing, and converting, energies inside you, and around you. The HEXAGRAMS will open your awareness to the situation in a symbolic (energy) way, to give you advice and guidance on the best use of your energy. By observing the HEXAGRAMS, and the way they change, the ancient Chinese were able to represent each situation, condition, or event, in life, and predict change. Each line of the HEXAGRAM, and your situation, has the potential for change because of the Four Dynamic Laws of Energy consumption and output.

ATTITUDE CONSUMES ENERGY

▬▬▬▬▬▬▬

AWARENESS CONVERTS ENERGY

▬▬ ▬▬

The Four Dynamic Laws of Energy

Inflowing Energy   **Outflowing Energy**

▬▬▬▬▬   ▬▬ ▬▬

1.   ENERGY PRODUCES ENERGY

▬▬ ▬▬   produces   ▬▬ ▬▬

Outflowing Energy increases energy output. This energy will
double itself, or, when not in use, convert back into

▬▬▬▬▬

2.   ENERGY FEEDS ON ITSELF

▬▬▬▬▬   feeds on   ▬▬▬▬▬

Inflowing Energy exists and thrives on itself. It uses-up whatever
energy is present and fills the gap with more Inflowing Energy.

3.   ENERGY FLOWS,
ADDS, DIVERTS, OR CONVERTS
It never stops or subtracts.
Energy is replenished by being converted or increased.

▬▬▬▬ + ▬▬▬▬ = ▬▬▬▬

▬▬▬▬ + ▬▬ ▬▬ = ▬▬▬▬

▬▬ ▬▬ = ▬▬ ▬▬ ▬▬ ▬▬

Energy will flow outwards and increase, or flow inwards to maintain itself.

4.   FLOWING ENERGY CAUSES CHANGE

▬▬▬▬   can become   ▬▬ ▬▬

▬▬ ▬▬   can become   ▬▬▬▬

34

Only you, even with a wide range of social influences, establish your own level of AWARENESSS. This awareness will increase and develop when you start to look at the world without your concern, and your inner thoughts of control or worry. You can take this step by not taking the world *quite so seriously.* When you accept yourself, and the world, without choice, obligation, or the need to control, you can let Outflowing Energy naturally follow its' course and provide more in your life. Outflowing Energy influences, allows, receives, and enjoys, and in this *it is automatic*.

By letting go of your tendency to immediate reaction, or your reliance on future rewards and promises, you open the gates for the energy to flow in a different direction. With Inflowing Energy you will always have to expend more energy to get what you want, while consumption and output increases the further away you get from your desired end.

You can have what you want, but there is an easier way to get it. That 'easier way' may not appeal because it appears to be going in the opposite direction. *All* energy flows in a powerful 'direction'. This flow of energy – TAO – takes you to where you are going, and most 'go with the flow'. The type of energy you use to achieve anything determines the direction of the flow of energy. In one direction, strengthened by your ATTITUDE, you are taken down the well-worn material route of experience, desire, reason and logic. Life is full of future hopes, past memories, successes and failures, rules, deadlines, and expectations. This is the life of involvement, which most will choose consciously or unconsciously. People want to be involved, concerned, and to react, but there is an alternative in inner peace and affinity.

The other directional flow, increased by observation and AWARENESS, follows an easier way of unexpected chances and spontaneity. Things change every day and every week. Anything can happen. Life is an adventure into the unknown. This is a life lived now, of contentment and ease, regardless of how busy you are, and, when you see it, the 'spiritual' in everyday life.

The automatic expression of energy provides you with the way. It also forms a HEXAGRAM, which you can select out of The TAO I CHING. The HEXAGRAMS of The TAO I CHING observe the world for you, and this is 'for your information only', and you can act on it, or not, later. Whatever energy you possess on an elemental level (in forming the HEXAGRAMS) can be guided by Outflowing Energy, thereby increasing your potential. By selecting a HEXAGRAM whenever you want you can embody, and make a reality of, Outflowing Energy. It is at this point, in the gateway of the moment, that you form the HEXAGRAM and enter TAO.

35

ENTER TAO

The Mystic Gateway

A Mystic Gateway is a sign, construction, element or situation, to alert you to the Here and Now. It can be physical, perceptual, or symbolic. Each time you go through a door, enter a room or building, or access another space, or another situation, you go through a gateway. No matter how grand, dramatic, or subtle, the gateway, its' mystic, or symbolic, purpose is to alert you to a shift in your present situation. There are many Mystic Gateways which you can physically step through, or enter through your five senses by observing the world, and through your imagination.

The Mystic Gateway of The TAO I CHING, was constructed over 3000 years ago and is still in use today. The HEXAGRAM symbols are constructed to awaken you to the present moment, through your situation. Your situation and involvement can be viewed in different ways, but the HEXAGRAMS tap into a flow of energy that materially and spiritually changes things. By using, through following the advice of, each HEXAGRAM you actually change your energy. Through this Mystic Gateway you embark upon a personal adventure of insight, awareness, enjoyment, and fulfilment.

A Mystic Gateway allows you to pass through into almost another dimension, where this everyday world is viewed in a very different way. A Mystic Gateway allows you to enter into another perception of reality. Mystic Gateways are open to all who 'take the time', and the effects are life enhancing and life changing, introducing you to a lighter, easier, and happier life.

The Gateway

is acknowledgement of your circumstances and situation and an acceptance of your personality and abilities, whoever you are. It is you who matters initially, not the rest of the world, and only you can make a difference. YOU are the gateway to TAO.

The Path

is the material world and your involvement in it, wherever you are. Through your choice of HEXAGRAMS you have a way of coping with obstacles and obstructions on the path. The obstacles are there to divert you, frighten, tempt, demand attention, and involve you. Do not have thoughts about the twists or turns in your path. These are not to distract you from *looking as you go along*. Without this awareness you are lost.

> *"The Way is always revealed before us if we care to see,*
> *but we get involved, distracted, and weary, and stop*
> *our journey before the end."*
>
> WANG PI

Your Guide

is simply your own well-being, happiness, interest, and fulfilment. Do not leave this to anyone else. This will sound selfish, so most will seek guides elsewhere.
You have 64 Helpers, who appear to you as HEXAGRAMS, and eight friends, in the form of the TRIGRAMS, who encourage and offer support, and sometimes tell you what you don't want to hear.

The Way

is a daily awareness of yourself in the present moment. You are very much a product of your own awareness and energy, *and you can change the type of energy you use* to dramatically change your life. Through the HEXAGRAM symbols you can discover your own energy level, and influence in the world. If you follow the advice of the HEXAGRAMS you will automatically change your energy output. This is all that is required to greatly increase your potential. Energy that is positive and outgoing increases in use. Energy that is negative or inward looking consumes more of that energy.

To those that use Inflowing Energy a change in approach towards simple observation will not come easy, for there are always a thousand and one things to think about, or chase after. If you are nervous or fearful, or even confident and assertive, you will certainly see enough in the world to keep you busy. The trick is to think less about what you must, need, want, or intend, to do, and more about what you are *actually doing now at this moment*. By all means retain your long and short term plans, but leave the present moment for living, *and looking about you now*. "Looking about you" is easy and automatic, but you could make this difficult or stressful by looking for something, concentrating, or focusing on your intentions, rather than what is *actually presented to you*.

The observation of what you see is out of your 'control'. You don't need to think about it. Just look and listen. The amazing thing that you will find is that it is the present moment that supports you, and shows you the way forward (and the HEXAGRAMS will help you here) through all manner of situations, events, people, and chances.

The more you employ Outflowing Energy, or allow it to flow through you, the more you let the world change for your benefit, and the more at ease you become. When you relax your hold on the world, and on others, the world will supply what you need for your well-being and harmony, whatever your circumstances. Each HEXAGRAM encourages this powerful effect, by setting your mind **at ease** before you step-out into the world. The HEXAGRAMS are constructed to do 'the thinking' for you, and present a solution through approach, awareness, or energy. By following the HEXAGRAM, you can retain a sense of trust and peace of mind under all conditions. Regular use of these HEXAGRAMS will change your energy flow.

TAO is the Way of living in the world, with others, and with yourself, with ease and inner peace. Letting your thoughts and concerns go, whatever the reasons, whatever the justification, or seriousness, even if only for a moment, brings about a great change. That change cannot be quantified, or put into a timeframe, and you will only see it or feel it as a quiet moment. From that quiet moment, which is always in the present, you may see the Mystic Gateways. Everything in the world changes, but here you are at the centre of that change. At the centre it is quiet. To find, or more correctly to be at, the quiet centre is to be enlightened.

"All the events in life are shown in the HEXAGRAMS. The HEXAGRAM symbols are not just flat, or relate to time and place, but possess an energy that extends into the Realm of Spirit. It is that which changes."

WANG PI

39

Releasing the Energy

When you select a HEXAGRAM you own it, and it becomes part of you for a moment, a day, or a week. It imparts the response you need to answer your question, or the particular energy to resolve or improve your situation. The HEXAGRAMS observe the world around you, and your own energy, in a lighter approach. The HEXAGRAM symbol changes with each individual, and in itself. The HEXAGRAM has a sort of constructive power that only operates when you select it and use it. At all other times it seems inert, and just another symbol.

The HEXAGRAM changes to fit *your* personality, and in that process of adaptation it starts to do its' job. To get the HEXAGRAM to work you'll need to 'try it on for size' *and actually use it in the world,* by trusting the advice. It may be like an overcoat for your protection, to keep you warm and comfortable in all weathers, or like a shirt or light top, for appearance, expression, or attraction. Perhaps it will take on a more formal appearance, to give you information, authority, or confidence.

 There are a number of ways to release the energy of the HEXAGRAMS. The most obvious is to read the text, and follow the advice. Each of the HEXAGRAM symbols has a message for you. For instance, HEXAGRAM 45 "FEAR" is an *illustration or symbol of a balance of energy* which contains the condition, cause, resolution, or consequence, of fear. If you select HEXAGRAM 45 "FEAR" you can 'activate' the solution by reading the information. If you have no cause to fear, and you come across HEXAGRAM 45, it will just direct the flow of energy towards overcoming a potential situation of fear. Since each HEXAGRAM promotes Outflowing Energy, that energy will simply flow straight through you. The HEXAGRAM contains all you need. Accept the advice, or the brevity of it, as appropriate, and don't be tempted to add more of your own thoughts, concern, or action.

However, there is a more direct way to 'assimilate' the energy of the HEXAGRAM, by 'associating' your breath with each line of the HEXAGRAM. If you know the number of the HEXAGRAM it makes it much easier to visualise each line of each TRIGRAM as you proceed. This is not a breathing exercise, merely an association with the rhythm of the HEXAGRAM. No thinking or concentration is required.

For each ▬▬▬ LINE *breathe in*

For each ▬ ▬ LINE *breathe out*

This is, to repeat, not a breathing exercise but an 'association of attention'. You pay attention to the breath required. If you also have to breathe in or out between the lines, as it were, when there are repeated lines for instance, this is permissible, and necessary. You breathe (or put your attention on) *energy in or out*, to bring it in, or to release it. By following the rhythm of breathing for HEXAGRAM 45 "FEAR", for instance, you will have the correct energy to handle the situation.

 Align your breath with the HEXAGRAM LINES. Starting at the top, breathe in energy, breathe out, and breathe in, to settle your emotions, thoughts, and feelings. Just concentrate on the energy coming in and going out. Now, breath in once, and let go of energy twice slowly in two out breaths, ignoring the fact that you may breathe in between these breaths. Take it slowly and deliberately. You are now in a state to face the world, with the correct amount of energy inside you. That association with calm breathing will give you an insight into the flow of Outflowing Energy.

Each HEXAGRAM is a symbol of the balance of Outflowing Energy, and each is pre-loaded with Outflowing Energy. Outflowing Energy is to be found in all those ▬▬▬ ▬▬▬ lines in almost every HEXAGRAM in The TAO I CHING, that stand for optimism, enthusiasm, encouragement, humour, and generosity. Situations and people will come under your influence quite spontaneously without your involved thoughts, and the pressure of Inflowing Energy. The HEXAGRAMS exist while you work, rest, and play, and continually change as you change, and when you see this, and can demonstrate it to yourself in an 'organised system', you'll have the key to TAO.

41

THE TAO I CHING

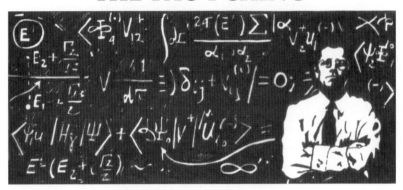

The Ultimate Calculation

TAO is the universal movement of energy. To see TAO in action, and to 'use' it, you will need a very spontaneous and flexible system. The ancient Chinese invented this too, as a spiritual way of coping with a material life of change. At any moment this flow of energy that runs through you, and the world, can be represented by a symbol *that is constantly changing*. All the movements and changes which affect your life have been calculated and represented in the 64 HEXAGRAM symbols of The TAO I CHING. Each of these six lined HEXAGRAM symbols represents a different situation, condition, or event, in your life. Take a look at this ultimate set of symbols, for it contains the shifting balance of energy throughout the day, the week, and throughout your life.

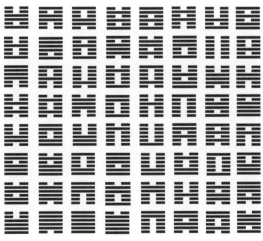

A typical
HEXAGRAM

43

The TAO I CHING provides advice, guidance, and direction, through an awareness of this flow of energy. The stance you take in your life has an impact not only on your own life and happiness, but on the actual condition and 'direction' of the world around you.

Normally, you are aware of the effect of outside events (the state of the world, society, family and friends), and from this you gauge your level of involvement (busy, inactive, independent, supportive). As well as this you will have an emotional response (a general feeling of progress or delay, confidence, dissatisfaction), and an overall daily 'perceptual picture' that includes the weather.

Your situation, your mental state, and your place in the world, is an energy interplay that interacts with the world. You cannot see these invisible energies, but when you look at a HEXAGRAM symbol you have one instance of this structure and balance of energy in a visible form. This is your energy in the world.

The HEXAGRAM is only a symbol, and as such, just a few lines on a piece of paper, but *it has the capacity to change, and through this change, show you the way forward.* Knowing this symbol at the correct moment, for it changes frequently, gives you the advantage of understanding and awareness, and an insight into the potential, diversity, and choice, available to you at each moment.

EACH HEXAGRAM MAY CHANGE AND DEVELOP AS A RESULT OF
A CHANGE OF ENERGY, DUE TO YOUR THOUGHTS, ACTIONS, OR CHANCE.

Energy is always moving, and it is the two directional flows of energy that 'rule the world', and influence and make up the construction of each HEXAGRAM symbol. It is these two different flows of energy, Inflowing Energy and Outflowing Energy, that combine or compete for balance or dominance in the World, and in Man.

The Rules of TAO

TAO IS PURE ENERGY

invisible, and manifested, in the world. The flow of energy is subject to the
dynamic interplay of

Inflowing Energy   and   **Outflowing Energy**

TAO REFLECTS YOUR SITUATION

through the HEXAGRAMS.

Each represents a different situation, condition, or event, in your life.

ACCESS   IMPROVEMENT   AMBITION   PROSPERITY

TAO IS AUTOMATIC

and does not require your control, or concern. Each HEXAGRAM
indicates your 'potential to succeed' through Outflowing Energy.

TAO DOES THE TIMING

of every event in your life from involved decisions, to your age.
All of these 'timed events' are for TAO to run after, not you.

TAO MOVES OR CHANGES

every 5½ days, or sooner. You will not normally see the flow of energy
unless you are aware of the Mechanics of TAO. You can, however, see
this happen, *before it happens*, in the CHANGING LINES of the HEXAGRAM.

TAO IS RULED BY CHANCE AND CHANGE

chance (connections) and change (movement)
through the TRIGRAMS

The TRIGRAMS are three line symbols that represent a fluid state, action, or
directional flow of energy.   There are eight TRIGRAMS, and each one shows
a different flow of energy, which will affect you, and your situation.

The TRIGRAMS

Each TRIGRAM is numbered, and has a title.

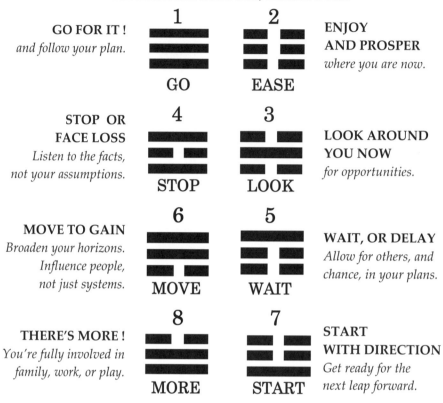

GO FOR IT !
and follow your plan.

1

GO

2

EASE

**ENJOY
AND PROSPER**
where you are now.

**STOP OR
FACE LOSS**
*Listen to the facts,
not your assumptions.*

4

STOP

3

LOOK

**LOOK AROUND
YOU NOW**
for opportunities.

MOVE TO GAIN
*Broaden your horizons.
Influence people,
not just systems.*

6

MOVE

5

WAIT

WAIT, OR DELAY
*Allow for others, and
chance, in your plans.*

THERE'S MORE !
*You're fully involved in
family, work, or play.*

8

MORE

7

START

**START
WITH DIRECTION**
*Get ready for the
next leap forward.*

**The TRIGRAM indicates the direction, a warning, or confirmation,
of your intentions or actions.**

TWO TRIGRAMS MAKE UP EACH HEXAGRAM.
The number of each HEXAGRAM is taken from the two TRIGRAMS.

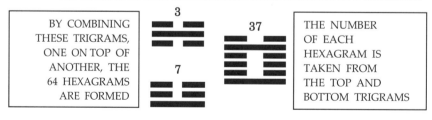

BY COMBINING
THESE TRIGRAMS,
ONE ON TOP OF
ANOTHER, THE
64 HEXAGRAMS
ARE FORMED

3

7

37

THE NUMBER
OF EACH
HEXAGRAM IS
TAKEN FROM
THE TOP AND
BOTTOM TRIGRAMS

The Advice of the TRIGRAMS

1

You have...
CONFIDENCE
DRIVE
POWER
CONTROL

Now you ...
ORGANISE
CONSTRUCT
FOCUS
CONVINCE

GO

AIM FOR GENEROSITY

2

You have ...
HARMONY
AWARENESS
SENSITIVITY
TRUST

So just...
RELAX
ENJOY
CREATE
SHARE

EASE

AIM FOR SPONTANEITY

4

You are...
STUBBORN
IMPULSIVE
DEFENSIVE
EXPLOITATIVE

Because of...
LOSS
REACTION
OPPOSITION
AMBITION

STOP

AIM FOR UNDERSTANDING

3

You have...
ACCESS
OPTIMISM
OPPORTUNITY
CHANCE

Just...
ACCEPT
OBSERVE
ADAPT
RESPOND

LOOK

AIM FOR SUBTLETY

6

You have...
STATUS
MOTIVATION
MOBILITY
INDEPENDENCE

You need to...
CONFORM
MANIPULATE
INSPIRE
PROMOTE

MOVE

AIM FOR INFLUENCE

5

You have...
DOUBT
DELAY
CONFUSION
INERTIA

So...
ASK
PERSIST
CONSIDER
CONSOLIDATE

WAIT

AIM FOR CLARITY

8

You have...
PLEASURE
INVOLVEMENT
INDULGENCE
IMAGINATION

And see...
DIVERSITY
ATTRACTION
EXCITEMENT
INTEREST

MORE

AIM FOR VARIETY

7

You have...
ENTERPRISE
DIRECTION
ENTHUSIASM
PROGRESS

Now...
PLAN
AFFIRM
IMPROVE
CHANGE

START

AIM FOR DEVELOPMENT

The Process of Change

The TRIGRAMS are not static. They do not represent character or personality traits, and they are not, whichever ones you are predisposed to, fixed at birth. The TRIGRAMS are flows of energy that can be adopted by anyone, consciously or unconsciously.

Through the combination of TRIGRAMS, each HEXAGRAM reveals not only your intentions, ways of coping and 'avoiding', but also the nature of the problem or choice you face, as well as the state of the world around you. The process of chance and change is known as TAO or 'The Way'. By responding correctly to the HEXAGRAM energy you may follow TAO and 'go with the flow'.

The energy of the TRIGRAM symbols *stimulate chance and change, and, once you have your HEXAGRAM, can be changed by you, or the prevailing energy, or chance.* You can use the TRIGRAMS to determine your direction in life, and to improve your performance. What do you want in life ? What do you want to achieve ? Select one of the TRIGRAMS from 'The Advice of the TRIGRAMS' chart on the previous page, to reflect what you want. Next, look at your own behaviour and actions at present, and ask "What am I actually doing ?", "How am I going about things today ?" Take a closer look at 'The Advice of the TRIGRAMS' chart and select ANY TRIGRAM that best describes your behaviour or approach, and place it under the first one.

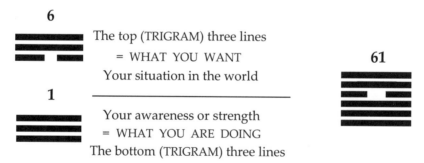

Now, by consulting the HEXAGRAM, you can see how things are proceeding. At some point you may consider a different direction in life – change the top TRIGRAM. You may feel the need, or be prompted, to alter your approach, perhaps more in line with what is happening, or for better results – change the bottom TRIGRAM. Consult the HEXAGRAM that you have now created. This is a way of using the TRIGRAMS as a process of change.

At first all the HEXAGRAMS will look much the same to you, until you pick out your favourites. You are not expected to know the title of each HEXAGRAM, but you can know the number of each one for quick reference.

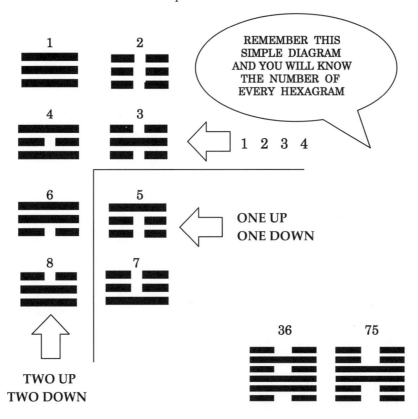

The energy level in you, and in the world around you, establishes a situation, which is reflected, and explained, by the HEXAGRAM. The HEXAGRAM shows the flow of energy (TAO) in the particular circumstances you face, *and will reveal, often deep, personal issues.* You may be given the solution to your problem, or the correct way to overcome an obstacle or handle a situation. At certain times in your life you may face a turning point and be shown other potentials and directions, and the energy required to meet them, rather than the simple question you want answered. At other times you may be given an insight into the actual process of change and an understanding of the power of Outflowing Energy.

How to use The TAO I CHING

1.

AT ANY TIME YOU CAN SELECT A HEXAGRAM TO ANSWER
ANY QUESTION ABOUT YOUR SITUATION OR INTENTIONS.

You can ask about any situation, or problem, or decision, and the advice is impartial, but geared to your energy. Generally, ask only for yourself and keep it personal, but not 'emotional'. When you seek advice or information, you'll need to compose your problem, situation, or alternatives, *as a question*. Focus on one topic at a time. It is usually best to select an option and ask about its' likely success or progress, and, depending on the answer, go on to other options and ask about them. The advice or information often answers deeper issues, which will be relevant to your situation. The timing of the response can never be 'forced' or presumed because the speed of events will be due to others, developing circumstances, chance, and your own innate 'speed' through life, rather than dates and times. Get your answer, and leave the timing to TAO.

2.

AT ANY TIME, OR AT THE START OF EACH WEEK, YOU CAN SELECT A HEXAGRAM
TO REFLECT AND INFORM YOU ABOUT YOUR POSITION, OR
ASSESS YOUR SITUATION AND PREDICT EVENTS FOR THE WEEK AHEAD.

Ask for yourself and situation to be blended into, and REFLECTED by, a HEXAGRAM. This is your message, understanding, or indication, for the week ahead. Providing you are calm and unhurried, the HEXAGRAM will always reflect your situation.

Ideally, you should select a HEXAGRAM every 5 days, or at the start of each week, in order to 'go with the flow' of TAO. During the week you'll need to be observant enough to see, act out, or understand, your HEXAGRAM, which will be hidden or revealed in different situations and circumstances each time. By this method you enter TAO, and will actually see the HEXAGRAM materialise. A HEXAGRAM should last you about a week, often quicker, sometimes slower when you or conditions are in a balance. If you consult the HEXAGRAMS on a regular basis your awareness and well-being will develop as you tune into the flow of Outflowing Energy. Each HEXAGRAM it is pre-programmed to change your energy output.

3.
GOING WITH THE FLOW OF TAO

There is a Way through the HEXAGRAMS which you can access by consulting the HEXAGRAMS in an order established by Wang Pi in 246 A.D. The order presented in this book (11 – 88) exists only to provide quick access to each HEXAGRAM. You could read all the HEXAGRAMS in the 'correct' sequence, 'cover to cover', in your own time. Read through each HEXAGRAM, at least a few times, as though you were in the situation, and seek the message, or understanding, at the point of change. This familiarization will give you an overall understanding of the process of change and give you an easier and more effective approach to the world, and to yourself.

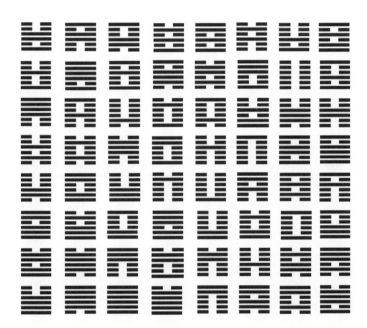

You can follow the HEXAGRAM sequence below (which runs top row to bottom row, left to right), and also as a route through the HEXAGRAM diagram above.

```
67 37 46 34 64 35 24 48 54 75 41 42 51 13 84 63
66 62 81 11 16 71 88 61 26 73 15 77 74 45 56 47
14 55 23 85 33 68 31 86 12 58 21 87 18 28 82 25
36 57 38 65 43 44 52 78 76 22 17 83 53 72 27 32
```

How to select a HEXAGRAM

You have instant access to all the HEXAGRAMS in The TAO I CHING with a special set of ELEMENTS ©. The order and sequence of all the LINES on all the ELEMENTS © are mathematically adjusted to give you the right HEXAGRAM every time, with an accurate reflection of all the potential CHANGING LINES.

The HEXAGRAMS represent **moving situations**, and THE LINES of each HEXAGRAM are constantly changing as a result of the moving situation, your energy, or chance events. If your situation, problem, or question, is likely to change and develop, a SECOND HEXAGRAM is formed through CHANGING LINES. These CHANGING LINES are indicated with a circle or dot.

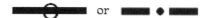 or

A SECOND HEXAGRAM represents a shift or development in the situation, a resolution, or future consequences. A SECOND HEXAGRAM is formed when all the CHANGING LINES are changed at the same time. If there are no CHANGING LINES the situation is relatively stable and there will be only one HEXAGRAM.

Selecting the HEXAGRAM is very easy, but you need to approach it carefully. If you have no real intention, or pose a very broad enquiry, or pretend an interest, you will get a chance response. *To answer specific questions, to solve a problem, help with a decision, or to reveal the, sometimes unseen, facts of a particular situation, you must select the HEXAGRAM carefully.*

Have a definite question in mind, about your intentions or situation, or a problem perhaps. Clear your mind of any thoughts other than the question. Do not expect, or prompt, any particular answer. You need to be relaxed and undisturbed. Even though these ELEMENTS © give you instant access, **you must** ensure that you are quiet and still, and have taken the time to compose yourself, when you select your HEXAGRAM, otherwise you will reflect your present energy, desire, anticipation, or control. Take your time. The spontaneous choice of HEXAGRAM may seem random at first but, if you give it your proper attention, it will encapsulate the present, the potential of the future, and the best use of your energy.

The eleven ELEMENTS © are be kept or stored in the bag.
Only you should use these ELEMENTS ©.
Do not let anyone else handle the ELEMENTS ©.

Think of your question while you select six ELEMENTS © from the eleven in the bag, and stand them squarely in front of you, upright-end-on. The closest LINE to you will be the bottom LINE of the HEXAGRAM.   For your first HEXAGRAM, ignore any dots or circles

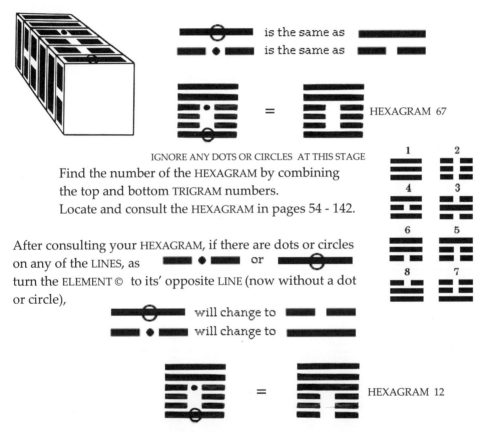

is the same as

is the same as

=   HEXAGRAM 67

IGNORE ANY DOTS OR CIRCLES AT THIS STAGE

Find the number of the HEXAGRAM by combining
the top and bottom TRIGRAM numbers.
Locate and consult the HEXAGRAM in pages 54 - 142.

After consulting your HEXAGRAM, if there are dots or circles
on any of the LINES, as   or
turn the ELEMENT © to its' opposite LINE (now without a dot
or circle),

will change to

will change to

=   HEXAGRAM 12

Change all the lines in one go, to form the SECOND HEXAGRAM.
Locate and consult this SECOND HEXAGRAM for the future development,
or resolution, of the situation.

If you do not possess a set of ELEMENTS ©, these can be obtained through the
taoiching.com web site, or you could just go to the back page now for the more
long-winded traditional Three Coin Method of selection.

The 64 Hexagrams

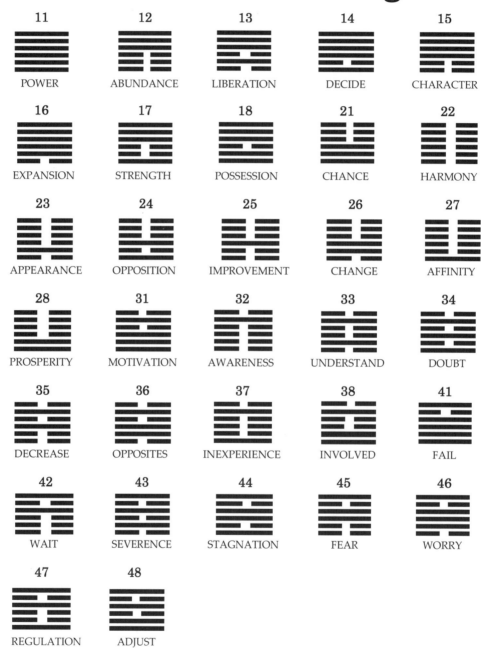

11	12	13	14	15
POWER	ABUNDANCE	LIBERATION	DECIDE	CHARACTER

16	17	18	21	22
EXPANSION	STRENGTH	POSSESSION	CHANCE	HARMONY

23	24	25	26	27
APPEARANCE	OPPOSITION	IMPROVEMENT	CHANGE	AFFINITY

28	31	32	33	34
PROSPERITY	MOTIVATION	AWARENESS	UNDERSTAND	DOUBT

35	36	37	38	41
DECREASE	OPPOSITES	INEXPERIENCE	INVOLVED	FAIL

42	43	44	45	46
WAIT	SEVERENCE	STAGNATION	FEAR	WORRY

47	48
REGULATION	ADJUST

# of The TAO I CHING

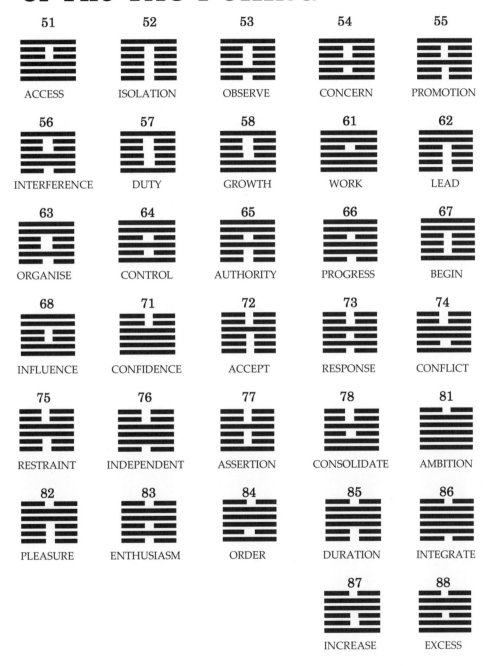

51	52	53	54	55
ACCESS	ISOLATION	OBSERVE	CONCERN	PROMOTION

56	57	58	61	62
INTERFERENCE	DUTY	GROWTH	WORK	LEAD

63	64	65	66	67
ORGANISE	CONTROL	AUTHORITY	PROGRESS	BEGIN

68	71	72	73	74
INFLUENCE	CONFIDENCE	ACCEPT	RESPONSE	CONFLICT

75	76	77	78	81
RESTRAINT	INDEPENDENT	ASSERTION	CONSOLIDATE	AMBITION

82	83	84	85	86
PLEASURE	ENTHUSIASM	ORDER	DURATION	INTEGRATE

87	88
INCREASE	EXCESS

11
POWER

You have the strength, confidence, and ability, to organise and control your situation, and with your drive and ambition you can expect success. This indicates that you are a committed, competitive, or involved person (usually 'self-made'), who has the power to realise ambitions in the world. Your success in life will be expressed through a drive or passion for personal advancement, in material or social terms.

Decide what you want out of life, plan for it, and go for it ! It's all in the determination, preparation, and persistence. When you have a plan, all events and people are aids to your progress, and 'opposition' or competition is there to be overcome or superseded. Watch the details, adapt existing systems to your ends, and exclusively maintain and promote your central idea. This is the way to achievement.

You have the power to change ideas, plans, or ambitions, into reality. Although opposition is to be expected, you are by nature highly competitive, and this often provides further impetus. It is your drive, or high energy, coupled with an intelligence at discerning trends and movements, loyalties and tactics, that secures your success. Your power rests in the manipulation of resources with decisive action. Your determination is best concentrated within a specialisation, or business skills. Be the expert. Convince people. Confidence, not the use of force, is the key.

DRIVE AND DIRECTION

12

ABUNDANCE

 You can expect a combination of material fulfilment and great satisfaction. You have more than your share of good fortune, sharing, and happiness. You can complete projects, consider a retirement, or find fulfilment in your imagination or creativity. There may be a 'change of gear' to inner pursuits and interests.

There are material developments and social activity. The more relaxed you are in your present position, the further you'll go. As you share, you increase.

Take this opportunity to look around you, and observe that power does not always rest in the obvious or the strong. What is new, young, or untried, has great potential. Adapt your knowledge, talents, and resources, to the existing situation around you. Be mindful of greed, or over-extending yourself, or of these intentions in others. The strictly personal use, or abuse, of good fortune will incur opposition or resentment.

There is a fortunate partnership. Possibly your knowledge and confidence is matched by another's practicality and influence, or vice versa.

COMPLETION AND HAPPINESS

13

LIBERATION

You have emerged, or are about to emerge, from a situation or circumstances that have been restricting you in some way. You now enter a new expansive phase. A complete change in circumstances is indicated, which can involve 'moving house', or having a fresh start in life. You've outgrown your situation and it's time to move on materially, emotionally, or  spiritually. This is essentially an inner call or desire to get more out of life. Plan and prepare for material changes and progress.

You could continue as before but it would eventually lead to a loss of credibility or potential. You have the capacity to change your situation and discard previous commitments or casual acquaintances, with whom you have no real connection. You may have to put some distance between you and others who do not entirely share your way of life. Remain flexible and adaptable, leave the past behind you, and face the future with some optimism. Do not confuse 'moving house' with the solution to all your problems. A change of location may not be the whole of the answer, so consider other aspects of your routine, behaviour, or 'idealistic notions', before you go any further. The objective is not to run away from things, but to run towards a newer and better life.

You may feel as though things are very much 'up in the air' and that you have no firm base, or that great changes are about to take place, but which you cannot see yet. Do not be alarmed. You will change as much as your situation and circumstances. You'll need to let go of the old, to get hold of the new. This is the end of a phase in your life. In some sense something is lost, while something else is gained. Accept, and discard, the past, as you look forward to a new future. Your influence in the world is about to be asserted, which up to now has been compromised. You are 'stepping out' of what you are familiar with, to go somewhere, or to do something, for a change. Practice by going for walks, or visiting places, in unfamiliar territory. Don't forget to dress for the occasion.

OLD   OR   BOLD

14

DECIDE

 You are unable to decide between the material demands, responsibilities, and commitments, of your position, or following your own direction and interests. Your indecision reflects a loss of focus or completion. If things were already complete and satisfactory there would be no decision to be made. You have come so far, but may have forgotten what your original intentions were. You may have been given to believe that your own 'selfish' needs are not justified or possible, when in fact it is precisely that quality of self-interest and self-determination that is needed here. Your self-interest is not in conflict with others if you do not impose, or rely, on others.

Others, of course, may not be so self-reliant or forgiving when they tell you that their self-interest comes before yours'. Your choice may have been based on your observations of the needs, or demands, of others, when really this is about your own life and happiness. Here is an opportunity, although presented in an awkward manner, to get back on track. Watch others, while you look to yourself.

The big question is, do you do what is expected of you and follow your duties and responsibilities, or do you please yourself ? The choice before you may be anything from active to passive roles, to material or spiritual paths, to community involvement or solitary work, or to helping others or yourself. Material progress is indicated, and yet you hesitate and doubt, even though at the back of all this is the notion or possibility that you could 'follow your dream'. As always, you can be delayed by heavy commitments, other offers, and further considerations. Free yourself from all this doubt and follow your heart, not your head. It is important to realise your situation. Just because you are capable, you are not expected to meet every demand, or continually contribute to others' lives, without any personal reward. Find your own level of working or involvement by taking note of your own interests, satisfaction, and feelings, and not to be so overly influenced by the demands or advice of others.

If your circumstances are reasonably comfortable, you should consider extending yourself a little more, either socially, creatively, educationally, or spiritually. That sense of comfort could lead to a sort of apathy or inertia, and you might not even suspect the cause. If conditions are awkward or difficult, these very circumstances divert your attention away from yourself. You must be happy to do what you do, otherwise you will continually be at odds with, and resent, the world, and others, around you.

The world could offer you a lot more, but you continue to hold-on, stubbornly or resentfully, to your notions. If you respond with reaction or crusades, you will be kept very busy indeed. There are lots of things wrong in the world, and with other people, and you need to decide whether it suits your health and interests to be a part of it, or so involved. If you follow your own heart, the consequences of abandoning the expected path of duty and responsibility, and being so fully involved in certain activities, can appear daunting and isolating. You may not be given much encouragement or support here, but you need to get out of the present situation, or your indecision over it's worth. Any indecision, unhappiness, stress, or demands placed on you, are the signs that something is wrong. You are a strong person so follow your own interests, insight, and education, so that from now on the world is going to have to follow you.

DEMANDS OR DREAMS

15
CHARACTER

 You have been judged by others and found 'wanting', or you judge yourself by your own or others' standards. This is misguided or ill-informed. All of this means that your actual personality or potential has not been recognised, or you have been unjustly blamed. The effect is that you are being stopped by others, or yourself. You must discard past notions and personal history for they are outdated and gone. You'll need an inner assessment now in order to face the future, with the prospect of happiness and success. The past, as well as the old standards and beliefs, must be left behind. If you discard all the old blame, past failures and guilt, and especially others' views of you, you will find that these have nothing to do with who you really are. Surprisingly, for it might not have occurred to you, or been dismissed, your character (nature, or way of looking at the world), is your greatest asset. *You are better than you thought.*

Alternatively, you may have independent qualities or an easy-going nature which you may now feel, either insecure about, or inclined to renounce, in order to get the same material benefits or lifestyle as others. This course of action will have bad consequences. You already have the ability to live life as comfortably, and as interestingly, as you wish. Do not be fooled by the outward appearances of anyone else's situation or lifestyle, or you will discover their true nature, much to your disappointment.

You need time for a little quiet self-reflection, and not the usual impulsive or considerate reaction. Everyone has their own agenda which they use to influence, or interfere with, everyone else. For some reason you wait 'to the side', or delay, or are far too considerate. Your strength of character is intact, but it may be underused, taken advantage of, or used against itself. Stop thinking about everyone else first. You should be aware of your own mind and body, your attitude (which governs everything), and your own sense of worth. Be guided by your own interests and enthusiasm in a light, relaxed, and easy approach. That's all you need right now.

STANDARDS OR SELF

16
EXPANSION

The world is full enough to offer you some great prospects, and there is the indication of a huge potential for you. In these times others will naturally have the same desire to succeed, so you should not be feint-hearted, and need to take progressive steps towards your aims. You have insight, imagination, or skills, so use them to achieve great things. Expansion invariably follows  an open or adventurous heart, through inspiration and enterprise. You will draw people in to your schemes, and success is assured. Your biggest problem, should it ever arise, would be hesitation, or indecision, over the choice of details or directions.

Your aims should be as far-reaching as possible, since there is the time and strength to realise them. You may have to overcome the barriers of tradition, convention, or attitude, to succeed, and this does require some subtlety and persistence. Some things you will have to accept, and occasionally walk around, but you have the time and space to do so. With your potential, the world will meet and supply whatever you confidently seek. You have 'staying power' when everyone else goes for the short-term benefits. Expansion and improvement is based on a strong foundation and enduring motivation.

It is your way of doing things that brings success. When you relax outward control, concern, or restricting expectation, you will succeed easily. In some ways, you only have to 'be there', knowing your aims, and the rest will come to you, since you already possess the right qualities. In some strange way, what you say, *is*. Inspire others, and yourself. Take your project or idea to the next step. It is this creative leap, spontaneous idea, or new thinking, that leads you to true expansion. Look for, and expect, new horizons and a major breakthrough now. When diversity and simplicity come together you know you are on the right track.

FOUNDATION   OR   ADVENTURE

17
STRENGTH

 You are an active person with strength and potential, and can expect independence, material and personal power, and a position of status, responsibility, or authority. You are able to control and organise your resources, and have an influence over others through your contacts, encouragement, support, or generosity. Often chance, or fate, directs events, and sometimes a little encouragement is all it needs to promote great changes. Use your talent in whatever area it lies, or organise through others. Your prosperity resides not only in many possessions but also in the influence you have with others.

With great strength there is always the danger that you may overlook the influences of chance and change. 'Transferable assets' will allow you to cope with the inevitable changes ahead, and in the present situation you should not over-extend yourself or take undue risks. Strength does not remove you from problems, only gives you the resources to cope. Observe conditions before you act, maintain a sense of proportion, and you will maintain your position of strength.

Making a show of strength certainly invites opposition. Using all your strength invites exhaustion, and your opposition might encourage this. You are capable of great things, and also great losses if you do not understand your strength. Strength is the quiet flow of energy outwards, not 'holding', or 'using'. You can afford to be gentle, understanding, and patient, for you have the time, energy, and resources, at your disposal. "Walk the land with your well-being".

INDEPENDENCE AND INFLUENCE

18
POSSESSION

Strictly personal ambitions, status, and involvements, are reflected in lifestyle. You accumulate to gain more control or pleasure. The possession of material things gives you the benefits of comfort, pleasure, and status, and the pride of ownership. Possessions require your attention, effort, and money, and with more material possessions, this will become an  over-riding commitment. How much time you spend on material things should be balanced not only by the necessity, reward or pleasure, they give you, but on the potential to develop other areas of your life.

You may be tempted to take advantage of an apparently easy situation, or to engage in some new prospect, without full awareness of the cost. For many this is a way of life. Just be aware of the cost of borrowing, or the use and loss of your time. The alternative is not 'less', but "use" (what you have). The suggestion here is that you may loose any sense of proportion in the distractions of status, lifestyle, and ownership.

By all means continue in the direction you are going in, but if more effort is required, consider the implications. You can do all of this comfortably if you are not obsessed with, or pressured by, time. The irony is that the more you 'let go' the more you gain in fulfilment and happiness. Nevertheless, there is material progress, and the considerable social and status advantages that come with it.

PLEASURE OR PURPOSE

21
CHANCE

 You, or, in some cases, your circumstances, are highly unconventional. Throughout your life you can expect repeated changes in your appearance, identity, location, or job, and to travel extensively. Many times you will welcome the change, diversity, and variety of your life, and at other times regret the lack of security that everyone else strives for. You will have to accept your strange fate and adapt as best you can, for if you do not you will have inner as well as outer problems. You are a naturally powerful person, but you need to accept, or develop, a spontaneity in yourself, and be aware of the presence of chance in your life. Chance and change rule the world, and you are especially well equipped to deal with this. Go on your own heart, not the opinions, conventions, or expectation, of others. The adventure is inside, and in your circumstances.

You are rather special, even though others will not notice, and even you may need convincing. You will probably start life socially or personally disorientated, and may even feel isolated from the rest of the mundane world. What you know and do is often seen as the opposite way around to most. Good fortune comes from chance and change, and your inner response and detachment. At some point you will gain worldly accomplishments and status. Your happiness and, if you desire it, your considerable material success in life, rests in the use of this 'different' attitude, approach, perspective or sensitivity. You will have talents in this area that will extend to psychic or spiritual awareness. [Even now, you can 'break the rules' and read HEXAGRAM 58]. You have an awareness and sensitivity of others, and of 'The Otherside' (the Spiritual Realm), that is more developed than most. This awareness or sensitivity puts you on a different level to most, and this is why you don't really fit in with family, friends, social and work associates, and partners until you find the right one. You have been born into this scheme of things with an awareness beyond the mundane, and have to sort-out what all of this means, and what you are doing here. If you haven't recognised or used your abilities yet, it is time you thought about it.

Viewed from the standpoint of most people you are 'an outsider'. That is, you don't quite 'fit in ' to everyone else's plans, notions, and agenda. Now you, particularly, are clever enough to cover this up with all sorts of 'regular' behaviour, getting-ahead, conforming and adjusting, so that you don't stick-out too much, and can pretend to be, or adjust to being, just like everyone else. If you've been very clever, or circumstances have kept you busy, you will have even convinced yourself that your present attitudes and involvements are very much a part of the everyday world. Forget it ! You don't fit in, and never will. (The modern day mystic can see people like you a mile away !) Fortunately for you, most people are dull-witted, or too busy, to see you for what you are, and they neither know, nor care.

Similarly, none of the things that they do have anything to do with you (strictly speaking). You must, if you are not already doing so naturally, exercise some self-control and be mindful of your approach to others. You do yourself an injustice if you think you can join-in with others on their level. Exercise prudent caution when dealing with others, since the world is in a state of fixed materialism and some may wish to take advantage of you. It is your sensitivity and awareness, your generosity and humour, not duty, possession, or status, that is your great strength.

Since you are a free spirit you may be inclined to seek change or adventure for its own sake. While you choose to change, do not be worried about your situation. You will not be affected by what you see, for you travel lightly. Whatever your circumstances, by being optimistic and observant, and ready for any offers, you will find that *the present situation will always sustain you*. This means that companionship and money are always provided when you need them. Remain confident, keep your own council, and the world will provide the rest. Being detached means acting without ulterior motives or heavy responsibilities, in a lighter and more spontaneous fashion. This is responding to the present moment rather than reacting to it. You have the option of a special route to happiness by-passing, as it were, the normal channels of involvement and social commitment. What you seek is much closer than you think. Your intuition or awareness is the link. Unlike others, you are able to draw strength from your control of desire, and you are well-disposed to take comfort in the knowledge that all security is an illusion. A sound heart, which you have, is all you require, and this you must develop, and take joy from. Make your heart, or feel it, comfortable and warm within you. *You* must do this. No one can do it for you, and you won't read about it in books. It's a sort of ease of attitude, an acceptance, and love of *all* things REGARDLESS of 'outside' conditions. You will then discover the contentment, of really being at ease with yourself, and your surroundings.

You might be inclined to be a 'loner', even though popular, and aware of your earthly circumstances as 'temporary'. No matter how well you do materially, or what possessions, or family, you acquire, you remain· "a stranger in a strange land". Since being a 'stranger' is a psychological, and even a spiritual, condition, it is important for you to understand, and come to terms with, your situation. You may never achieve that emotional dependence that everyone else calls 'Home'. You may, if you are lucky, experience this once in a lifetime, but only for a very short period, before your true 'independence', or nature, reasserts itself. You may not like this, but that's the way it is. Your 'home', or place, is on a spiritual level, not an emotional or geographical one. So, your main directive from now on is to make yourself "at home", or comfortable, WHEREVER you are. This you will find pretty easy, *once you know*, and it will be very rewarding, especially with a detached (spiritual) attitude of acceptance of places, and people. Your home is where your heart is, and your heart is portable, so it could go anywhere. To "a stranger in a strange land" it matters not what country, or domain, you are in. The possibility of taking (perhaps temporary) residence in 'foreign territory' is one that should not be overlooked. Circumstances may point you in this direction and, if you accept the invitation, you might well find a very satisfying and successful outcome.

Your confidence comes from an acceptance of chance and change – the very forces that influence the world. It is in the unexpected that great fortune comes. You will maintain your own integrity and, surprising to you, will manage to acquire property and the respect of the community. Greater still, you will find a partner of like-mind. Your greatest assets are persistence and optimism. Use them !

You cannot rely on your emotions to guide you, or 'the world's way of doing things', or other people, or the idea of wealth and security as the answer. They have no real meaning, only control and coercion. Fate, and chance and change, are on your side, so have some trust in TAO. You have a greater sensitivity and awareness than most. Trust that intuition ! You now live a spiritual life, in a material world, and this puts you on a different level to almost everyone else. You are a free spirit, that owes no allegiance to anyone or anything. Find that odd, or unsettling ? What you choose to support or love is up to you, no one else. As to the rest of it – deal with it, or enjoy it. NEVER REACT. Never say anything negative, no matter what the actual 'facts' are. It takes a little practice, and maybe a lot of 'catching yourself out', but it will become second nature to you, and it will change everything. All of this is important to you. By your words you are judged (you can think what you like). Always say the best. Adapt to all the circumstances you find yourself in, and at the same time enliven all situations with your enthusiasm, generosity, peculiar talents, and detachment. It's an odd balancing act, but a rewarding one.

From now on, and *this will sound odd until you do it,* whatever you want, just 'put your order in' for it. TAO will provide what you need to be comfortable, either spontaneously in response to the flow of your energy, or in response to 'an order' that follows that same energy. When you 'place an order', you do not ask for what you require. This is not asking, visualisation, affirmations, or chanting. If you ask for, want, or desire something, you will get a reflection of that energy, or the continuation of the circumstances that promote more desire.

To 'order' you will need to use your imagination. Imagine a telephone, *and in your imagination* pick it up, and *assume someone is listening.* This opens all the channels of communication, as you act as though you were talking to someone (or something). Place your order by describing the item you want, and stating that you want it. It's as simple as that. You could even end by saying "Thankyou for listening". Order once (repetition may help on this one occasion, if you want to make your point), then stand well back. What you 'order' will be offered to you through the world, freely, usually within six months. If money is required for the item you have ordered, it will be provided just for this thing. You are not to concern yourself with the How and When, or Where, for that is for TAO to run after – *not you.* The point is that you should not restrict yourself to what *you think* is possible. No thinking is required. Define, or describe, what you want. You could jot it down on the back of an old envelop first, to clarify your selection, and then 'put your order in'. As you place your order be specific, but not demanding. This is not about belief, or expectation (as such). What makes it work is simply the 'permission' to do so. You cannot give yourself permission through reason, need, reward, or faith, but only in a trust in some strange process called TAO. Most cannot, and will not, do this 'on their own'. You can.

There are some simple rules. Order any *thing* you want. You cannot, for instance, order status, or success, or happiness, only material things, objects, items, or possessions. Of course, things don't make you happy, but they will make your life easier. Love and happiness, expression and acceptance, are something that each person must sort out for themselves, and this could be a little easier if everything else was in place. Similarly, you cannot put an order in for money, only the things that money will buy, i.e. objects, possessions, or things. The monetary value, or size, of what you 'order' is immaterial. You can order as many things as you like, it won't make you any less 'spiritual', unless you take it all too seriously. Whatever you order is not taken from anyone else, and there is plenty there for you. You cannot 'order' things for others, even though you may see others in need. As to the wants and needs of others, they must find their own way, and you can (only) help through your support, love, enthusiasm and encouragement, or your psychic or spiritual work. You should not order things to impress, or harm, others. Desire or greed won't work on this level. This is primarily about your own well-being and comfort. You see, this is not about being spiritual, selfless, helping others, or exercising some sort of 'power', it is merely you and your own comfort, and interests.

To 'prove' all of this for yourself, make a list of what you want (without thought of the possibility, or monetary value). Spend a little time on your list until you are happy with it, then prioritise the list (what you want most, as №.1, etc.). That 'prioritising' is close to the frame of mind required to put an order in, in that choices are made on personal 'likes' rather than possibility, value, or practicality. 'Put your order in', (read your list as though selecting from a menu in a restaurant, in the same manner as above). Put your list away in a safe place, and stand well back. Cross off the items as they are delivered to you (which will be in any order). After six months all the items should be crossed off your list. If not (and you will know the reason for any delayed item), start another list, with these items on the top, if you still want them. It shouldn't take you very long to be in a position where you have everything you want, although this is an endless process, so you'll just order things as you need them. 'Putting your order in' is about what you want to make yourself comfortable. It is not about what you need, or 'must have', or require for status or ambition. Once you see this as 'an impersonal process', you will appreciate how much you are on such a different level to just about everyone else.

The greatest happiness is through friendship, and it is your birthright to have companionship, at whatever level you want it. Just 'order', as above. However, in much the same way that you cannot order money, so too, you cannot order named individuals, only the person who is right for you. In relationship matters it is often best to disengage yourself completely from unsatisfactory people before you 'order' someone else, since **this aspect is very powerful** when 'activated'. Once again, you should be specific, (describe the qualities you want), but not demanding (a particular named person). You can 'put an order in' for a new friend, a partner, a companion, 'soul mate', or spiritual advisor, or, if you're clever, all of them rolled into one. A (new) person will turn up within six months. Just be sure you know what you want, and you are ready for the relationship. In the same way that things, possessions, or objects, are there to give you pleasure or comfort, and not just to be used to impress, so too, partnerships are an aid to your own personal fulfilment, not a stepping stone to status or security. The object here is *to share*, not to work-out personal problems, or answer insecurities.

You do have a 'spiritual mission'. Just about everyone carries a burden on their back. This is just one way of sensing 'heavy' energy. You can lighten their load *for a short while*, through the use of your psychic talents, or simply through your encouragement, enthusiasm, generosity, and friendship. Sometimes it's just a smile, or a kind word, sometimes an 'unseen' thought of love, or healing, to someone you know, or to a total stranger. It can take a minute, or an hour, or more. In any case, most will go on their way, or resume previous habits, and without any thanks. You must 'let them go'. You are not to concern yourself further. In the same way, *you are to let the world go*. It is not your concern. Just do what you are able. What you see of the world should be what you know - that profound joy, quiet, the quality of light, the weather and time of day, and, when you see it, The Way in humans. Take the 'chances' that are offered to you, and the opportunities and strange turns of fate or direction, and even the misfortunes, with enthusiasm and gratitude. *This* is the great adventure.

All of this is very special. It is for you only when you select this HEXAGRAM, which will last a lifetime. Others will read this, and not believe it, or understand it.

FATE AND FORTUNE

71

22

HARMONY

 Above everything in this world is friendship. You'll have love, marriage, good friendship, or close partnerships. There is a state of harmony, and pleasant and progressive conditions are indicated. Amazingly, you find advantage in what is closest to you, or in the most unlikely of situations, or in the least promising of persons. Happiness is much closer than you think. By being at ease, and not in competition or conflict with your situation, you will find that there is a certain spontaneity to events.

Harmony and deep relationships require, not so much an element of surrender or compromise but, a lightness of ease and acceptance. As you progress you will attract others. You are able to influence people and situations with your quiet confidence. There may well be a 'chemistry' between you and your partner that could mean extra benefits in social terms, or rewarding enterprises. Through faith, or trust, there is a spiritual harmony that finds expression in your daily life. You should be looking forward with plans to 'go further' in the world. Do not hesitate to be adventurous, or to travel, if this is called for.

REFLECT   OR   SHARE

23

APPEARANCE

There is the appearance or notion of beauty, strength, agility, or ability, which may show itself in anything from being 'good looking', to a sporting or practical nature, to being involved in 'show business' or salesmanship. This will involve a talent, skill, a natural expertise, or relaxed confidence, often expressed as a passion, hobby, or profession. Your  performance, possibly in more than one sense, is the key to your success.

Take care of your appearance, for it will be an important factor now, and in the future. Make the most of what you have, but never take it too seriously, even though your livelihood or identity may depend on it. If you are tempted by excess, vanity, or complacency, it will be your downfall. A sense of proportion will ensure your future contentment.

Appearance can also be an illusion, usually intentional, for gain or enjoyment, as in deception or acting. Appearances also extend into lifestyle and environment, which may reveal much of a person's inner worth or motivation. There is always the possibility of dishonesty, exploitation, or ulterior motives. At this time do not trust words, looks, or books. Tread carefully, but confidently.

With regard to your own talent, you may have considered the 'easy way out', as it were, by doing what everyone else does. You, however, may be different, so consider the possibility of something new or original. It may take a few attempts, but have faith in your ability and insight. You may have over-looked the possibility of a hidden or unused talent that will answer your needs, provide access to wider horizons, or introduce you to others. Your contacts from these dealings or activities will be important for other aspects of your life. It may be time to achieve recognition in your chosen field.

ACT OR TACT

24
OPPOSITION

You don't want to conform. You oppose some established, conventional, or traditional way, authority, or order, that is firmly entrenched in the world. There is a possibility that you may even be reacting to, or resenting, your own situation or circumstances, or you lack the control you desire. It is your dissatisfaction that causes the opposition. This leads to the discovery of even more obstacles in front of you, and the more you react, the more diverse the problems become. Aggressive assertiveness, complaint or criticism, will get you nowhere. You maintain an attitude, mode of behaviour, or ambition, which stimulates this opposition. Persistence is one of your main qualities, so you must be very careful, for you could use all your time and energy sorting-out problems. In the present circumstances your own opposition means concentrated, but ultimately wasted, energy, and a lack of knowledge of the source, nature, or the power, of the opposition.

The situations or people that you face, and oppose, are far stronger, and more established, than you, so your approach or tactics need to be carefully considered. The situation is already fixed and functioning very well on its' present level. As you see it, your intentions and ambitions are blocked. You use a lot of energy to solve problems, to overcome obstructions, and to convince yourself that you will not be beaten. Let's face it, it's you that's not happy here, whatever you might say about the situation and others. You cannot change or control others, but you can have an influence if you consider change within yourself .Happiness or contentment is reached simply by agreeing (with yourself, or others) to seek pleasure and fulfilment. Compromise and solutions follow this easy intention. This means that there is an easier way to solve this conundrum. "Make yourself comfortable" in whatever way you can. Only you can do this for yourself. A change of attitude, rather than physical or material things, generally secures what you want. "Mind your own business !" (only). This is advice, not a rebuke.

It is not by presenting an opposite view, or by force, that you combat a superior opponent, or entrenched situation, but by enduring 'opposition'. That opposition must present *a very different way of doing things,* and this should be equitable, easy, or rewarding. If not, you engage in an endless fight, since hostility, in yourself or others, is intentional, reactive, or resentful. Material and physical reaction in this situation is useless, for the 'opposition' feeds on this. When this polarity is recognised it is only then that success is likely, but this takes time. For this reason, before you start, make sure that you are comfortable with what you propose, or intend to do, and that, even now, you are contented to do what you do.

To thrive on opposition is not the answer, and yet, for some, this is the solution to identity and control, and the consummation of a certain kind of energy. The advice which is not heeded here, leading to a continuance of the problem, is 'change yourself first, before you take-on the world'.

DEFEAT OR DEFIANT

25
IMPROVEMENT

 A change in your circumstances leads to a big improvement in your situation. There may be a new romantic relationship, which may be unexpected, and a development in your responsibilities or involvements. This change is the result of the actions of others, and your connection to them. You need to forget the past, or your previous over-cautious behaviour, although sensitivity is required in order not to upset certain balances or individuals. The situation unfolds in its' own time.

You will be offered some sort of assistance through a relationship, or friendship, which will help you establish your later independence. This points to an improvement in the quality of your life, your happiness, and continued progress. This development, either through chance, good fortune, or generosity, does provide you with the confidence to go forward, and to do other things. Look for improvement now, not just wish for it.

INVOLVEMENT   OR   FULFILLMENT

26
CHANGE

Be ready for some big changes, events or developments, ahead of you, some of which may be unplanned, or come unexpectedly early. There is a, possibly complete, transformation of your situation. If you accept this, you will adapt and prosper, but if you cannot accept this, you may face obstructions, setbacks, or apparent disappointment. If there 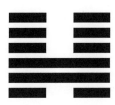 are no fixed expectations, or self-imposed conditions, and you take the opportunities that are offered, you will succeed where you thought it not possible. Good fortune comes in many forms, and often when, or where, you least expect it. Your potential is realised when you go with each situation. The simplest, and easiest, solution is often the answer.

In a mundane sense, there will be big changes in your social, career, or personal life, that allow you to go forward. On a deeper level, these changes are the mechanics of TAO, to offer you greater awareness and spiritual development. Chance and change are the greatest threats to our well-thought-out plans, the status quo, structures, and standards. You, however, must have enough awareness, to make the most of the situation. You may have to adopt, or adapt to, new rules, methods, or approaches. You may not be able to hold on to previous conditions, attitudes, or possessions, but the surprise is how well you do without them.

You may be about to discover something beyond order and material security – optimism. Optimism somehow instigates chance and change, but this is something you'll never believe, unless forced to by circumstances, or until you actually see it in action. Look out. This is optimistic advice, not a warning.

ADAPT   OR   OBSTRUCT

27

AFFINITY

This is a time for you to create, and enjoy, your place in the world. You have the potential to be 'at one' (or 'at home') with someone, something, or someplace. This could be 'finding your home', your own level, your place in society, or a spiritual state of detachment. Affinity is an acceptance, and an understanding, or compassion, or delight, in what is presented to you. You need do no more than look at what is offered.

To gain this affinity you must first accept things as they are. This means not being overly concerned about your situation, or anyone else's. You may have compassion for others, or about the state of the world, but you need to stop thinking and worrying about what should be, or what could be. Let situations, and people, 'unfold' as they will. This is for TAO to sort-out, not you. From being relaxed and at ease with the world *as it is,* comes an inner quiet or peace, whatever your circumstances might be. This is a blend of contentment and trust or faith. This inner peace is not just a mental state that is achieved in meditation, although this is so, but a way of 'being' in the world. This is a quiet way of coping with a world of action, diversity, chance and change.

From this inner peace you may engage the world on any level you want. Act simply as the situation requires. All you have to do is look out optimistically each day. The entire world and its' contents are provided for you to enjoy life, or to be fulfilled. Of course, chance and change, and misfortune, happen, but if you don't react, your awareness and acceptance gives you an affinity. When you can simply observe the world without justification you will be truly contented. There is, for you, a 'formula' that includes, and entwines, you and the present moment. It is "Enjoy Now". Now, or time, is inexplicably linked to here, or place. You can extend this awareness into the spiritual by looking 'symbolically' at the lightness of the world, through the simple observation of the quality of light, space(s), and the weather. This will present a whole new world to you. The results can be profound, and affinity can be seen as the most rewarding 'spiritual or detached' state in this material world of ours.

DETACHMENT AND DELIGHT

28
PROSPERITY

Success. A time of celebration. Sometimes wealth or good fortune may come unexpectedly, as a win or inheritance, or through your own endeavours. You may gain substantially from the labours of others, or your connections, or position. In such circumstances, you are in a position to enjoy much, and benefit those around you. Your only concern will be how to  cope with all of this, so try to keep things on a personal and manageable level.

Prosperity resides not only in wealth, but in the influence this gives you. This influence is not about status, possession, or exclusivity, but trust and support, and generosity. This is the difference between static possession and improving prosperity. Do not let wealth and happiness degenerate into the mere accumulation of material possessions and status, and the opposition, reaction, or exploitation, that may come from this. You will have the resources, so use them wisely to extend your good fortune.

A great idea, or a pleasant situation, will need you to add some vitality, attraction, style, or enthusiasm. Invest in some idealistic project or realise 'a dream' now.

REWARD OR DIVERSION

31
MOTIVATION

 You can profit materially from your ideas, schemes, strong motivation or drive, and, with your inspiration and intelligence, there is a lot more to come. This is the time for converting your speculative thoughts into reality. So, you need a plan, otherwise your circumstances will dictate your every move. Strategy or 'getting things done' is your 'forte'. With a strong sense of identity, you will already be pursuing your plans, or you can be guided by your talent, abilities, and interests. It is your motivation that is driving things at the moment, and the world awaits your best plan.

Motivation is usually based upon need, greed, or envy, when outer conditions attract, or provide the impetus for action, and a lack of it can lead to disillusion, apathy, or resignation. The secret of lasting motivation is to base it upon an idealistic, personal or mental, drive, in some senses almost regardless of worldly or financial issues.

Motivation is that *little glimpse at what is possible, and sometimes what is impossible.* Don't overlook the assistance of others, or simple good fortune. You can always benefit from looking at other avenues, systems or methods, or markets, that you may not have considered before. Each idea has a product, and each word has an effect. Copy and use !

You may be suited to an unorthodox approach. Consider non-traditional or unconventional avenues. Intuitive, creative, inventive, or intellectual, pursuits will open doors. There is also scope for artistic, cultural, or perhaps serious academic, work. Take it all *much further !* When you look back you'll wonder why you didn't, and subsequently missed all those chances. It is now time to act, and set things in motion.

CONVINCE OR CONVERT

32
AWARENESS

Intuitive, perhaps even spiritual, capacities are indicated. Your sphere of activity is to be found in your power of influence, through movement and change, since you persist under any conditions. This means that you have a certain sensitivity or awareness, or a sense of enthusiasm, or optimism. By simply trusting in your own abilities, by maintaining your sense of  confidence through a relaxed manner, you can achieve almost anything. That which you seek is already present within you, and anything else you require may be gained apparently with little effort. By observing the ways of the world you are able to mimic these and share in the benefits. Physical and material aspects are not to be overlooked, but neither can they become a prime motivation without incurring either stress or opposition. This is not your natural element. Your strength and power lies in creativity, spontaneity, and enthusiasm, and in a quiet persistence or acceptance.

You act as the situation requires, without emotional diversion or loss of energy through undue expectation. You are certainly talented or versatile in many areas. By an acceptance of your circumstances you will find true peace and personal power, but this requires sensitive awareness. It is your own heart, or your own level, and not the material world, as such, which brings you happiness. When you, and you alone, know what you want, let this be your guiding light in all things. When you decide what you want out of life, allow the situation or circumstances in the world to present the way forward.

You are one of those rare individuals who possess a high degree of awareness or sensitivity. This may, if you are not diverted or disturbed by your sensitivities, lead to a great understanding, and material rewards. In some senses, this is the opposite of the power that comes from identification and control. It is your job to trust TAO enough in any situation to find a way to express your enthusiasm and enterprise. Quite often you must be reticent, if not silent. You may not be the person who is obviously in charge, with the attendant rewards (and restrictions), but you will have great influence. Observe all that you are exposed to without over-reacting, without doubts, and adapt as you go along. Enthusiasm is the key.

Awareness can lead to great spiritual progress, if this is your aim. In short, your personal and inner development is assured. The longer you remain quiet in the wider social or commercial field, the more you can develop your own personal powers. Always proceed with a quiet confidence and do not doubt. That's all you ever have to do is live daily, with trust and spontaneity. You may well get the recognition you deserve, and a reputation in the world.

It is time to open, and go on, your own heart and intuition. Sometimes you won't know if you're being spontaneous or guided, but not knowing is your key to acceptance. You are about to exceed your expectations, or attain a higher level of understanding or awareness.

SPONTANEOUS   OR   GUIDED

33

UNDERSTAND

You have the ability to see both sides of an argument at the same time. With your intelligence, you can have a detached over-view of the diversity, conflicting interests, and the many options open to us. You know how others feel, what they want, and that they do behave in different ways. This is a rare gift. Your quiet confidence inspires or affects others. Even  though 'relating', counselling, communication, and teaching, are open to you, you must make sure you do express your own notions and understanding, and achieve your own goals in life. Whatever you do, you can rely on your intuition to guide you. When you understand what is going on, with your insight and confidence, you will achieve many things not possible to others.

Your approach should be, what may look passive but is, by active observation. Let others, or the situation itself, inform you. People of 'a like-mind' attract each other, and people attract to themselves the situations, relationships, and environment, that reflect their nature or involvement. By not interposing your view or beliefs, you will understand much. By such an 'impersonal' or detached acceptance you will also see your own way ahead through situations and circumstances as they are presented to you.

You need to be well-prepared for forth-coming events, for you may be causing, or 'opening-up', changes in others, or yourself. It would be wise to keep your skills and sensitivities on a practical, informative, and even professional, level, and not get too emotionally involved. You'll need your 'own space', at certain times, to function comfortably. Be careful of stating the opposite case, or another viewpoint, for the sake of it. Say what you know, only if asked, or when prompted by the situation. Remember to follow your own path, and leave others follow theirs'.

DIVISION OR DISCUSSION

34
DOUBT

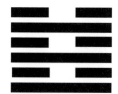 The message is simple, 'just decide what *you* want !', but you have taken it to great personal lengths. Your doubt or uncertainty conditions everything because you have given it so much prominence. This inner uncertainty leads to outer insecurity. You are uncertain in your own thoughts, desires, or intentions, about what you think you want, or what you think others want. Your reactions and considerations make choices or decisions almost impossible. Out of this impasse there is no escape. Your reasonable and modest disinclination to make decisions on, perhaps, insufficient resources or information shows, not prudence, or even a lack of direction, but a lack of interest and enthusiasm. You've been going in the wrong direction, and continue on the same course. This kind of self-doubt is not due to a lack of information, or ability, or the presence of uncertainty, but simple enthusiasm.

Nothing is absolutely certain in this world, apart from your present attitude and behaviour, which is limited by defeating personal frustration, or resentment. If you had the confidence, or simple desire or interest, you could make any decision, or follow any course of action, even on 'insufficient information', by doing the best as you see it with what you have now. Confident people simply do this all the time, because they follow their heart or instinct. You can take introspection too far, or wait the whole of your life to get all the facts, or for you and conditions 'to be just right'. There is a law that states, "If you don't do it now, you probably never will". This is a law that can be broken, but seldom is.

Doubt is healthy enough, until it stops you acting. Doubt as much as you like, but when you know what interests and motivates you, you can get on with things anyway. If you make a mistake you will soon know about it – and just change it. The job of doubt is to stop any movement and change. Doubt is often 'sparked-off' by a set of personal incidences or conditions which make you question your capabilities, or your ability to succeed in life. This is not really the issue, but you have made it one. Doubt is the fixed response to a whole range of conditions and experiences, that lead you on to endless re-appraisal and worry. This mental response is the cause and continuance of your present dilemma.

Your situation can not be solved by more concern, or more information. Continued worry, disappointment, and endless thinking, only increases the problem, and encourages the type of energy which is used to create even more problems. The amazing fact is that doubt is the opposite of enthusiasm. Doubt is not the opposite of knowledge, as might be commonly supposed. More information, better conditions, or even more money, will not help you here. How odd this will sound to you, with your desire to sort yourself out, or sort-out worldly conditions. The problem is not about meaning, or materials, but your inability to be happy. Movement must come from within, otherwise it is just another reaction. Your expression of enthusiasm and optimism can only come from deciding what you want. Find your interest. Express your interest.

It is time for a change. Find out what you are really interested in and enthusiastic about, regardless of convenience, competition, or others. You don't need a reason to enjoy yourself. This is a natural expression. Don't let 'perfection' get in the way, or past disappointments bring a halt to future happiness. "Enjoy Now" is a directive that you need to consider. Not only find your passion, interest, or comfort and ways of enjoying yourself, but do them now, not later. Doubt and delay go hand in hand. This is all about interest and enjoyment, not direction, duties, or any end result.

START OR DEBATE

35
DECREASE

 A loss of status, or health, forces you to readjust your position and priorities. You may over-react with a loss of motivation or hope, or over-compensate with stubborn or impulsive behaviour, but it is your view of yourself that needs adjusting. This is a period of 'enforced quiet', or there are events or circumstances that obstruct or delay your progress. While you seek to redress the balance of how things were, you only become more aware of your loss. Such a reaction is to be expected but it only leads to further decrease.

This is the time to take note of what you do have – inner strengths, talents, enjoyments, or support – not what you have lost. There is a need to look closely, and quietly, at your present surroundings, and adapt. You need less reaction, not more. A change to a lighter attitude may 'save your life'. This lighter attitude is the opposite of your normal attitude, or what is expected, but it's one you may be pre-disposed to, much to your surprise. This is a time of re-evaluation, and eventually the need to take new steps. Against all the odds and expectations, the decrease actually leads to greater fulfilment.

This 'decrease' is preventing you from using your energy, or using it too soon, or too much, or in the wrong direction. 'Holding on', or 'being a fighter', does not give you more strength. Inner strength comes from inside when you let go of, or ignore, outer conditions. What you will discover is, that when you 'let go', you only land HERE. Let the energy of events 'flow through you'. Do not hold on, but be ready and willing to let go, to adapt, to accept, and to go with this flow, regardless of the circumstances and the advice of others, and even your own notions.

You have tended to rely on worldly conditions or involvements, or an easy or busy lifestyle, but now things have altered in order to force you to consider your own inner development. A serious question of worth or purpose may arise. Whatever the cause for the decrease, your new situation will actually show you the way forward if you let it. Odd as it may seem, you have now been given a chance, through circumstances beyond your control, to develop and refine your character, or come to terms with who you really are. Do not loose this chance by simply taking the situation at face value, or as 'bad luck'. This 'decrease' will give you time to reflect on a new direction in your life. That new direction, and its' insights, will surprise you, and could be life-changing, even if you do get the chance to resume where you left off.

QUIET   OR   PANIC

36
OPPOSITES

 Sometimes chance events or people offer you the chance to greatly improve your situation. This contains the possibility of change. You will come into contact with your opposite. This is, most likely, a sexual partner, or it may be someone who could have a lasting influence on you. There is an element of attraction here, but, briefly on first meeting, there may be a negative impression. However, in a different light, things progress. Your opposite need not be in opposition, but merely express another (opposite) viewpoint. Essentially you are dealing with an independent person or situation which may co-exist with you if an understanding can be reached.

The course you take very much depends on how receptive and flexible you are. Lots of talking here leads to a relationship of mutual trust and advancement, and this may be what you need right now. You could double your strength and happiness. Just let nature take its' course, and relax your expectations and attitude.

Opposites attract, or react – you decide. Unity increases power and pleasure, while competition and conflict are time and energy consuming. With adaptability on both sides, the combination of forces can form a balance where both may express their potential at different times. You'll need a common purpose, so that each may contribute their best, in their own way. You could find mutual advantage and support here, and greatly increase your prospects.

COMPETITION OR EXPANSION

37

INEXPERIENCE

You are in the early stages of an enterprise, or there is a new start in unfamiliar territory. You lack experience, knowledge, or full awareness, of the situation, and yet this doesn't stop you. There may be concerns to which you over-react, or you may rely on your emotions to guide you. Control your emotions, or they will control you. The danger signals are stubbornness, reckless action, or taking-on too much. If you were to continue without motive, or care, or consideration for others, it would get you nowhere, or into great difficulties. Impulsive action, over-confidence, or premature ambition, in the present circumstances, without waiting for the right time, solution, or advice, would be unwise. The positive side of all of this is a 'learning period' that has a big impact on all aspects of your life.

There is a need to temper your ambitions or expectations. Most things do take time – from completing tasks to gathering experience. Think only of short-term objectives because, in the long term, things will change considerably, beyond your present expectations and awareness. The right approach is through a 'light-hearted' discovery, or learning skills, which can be a lot of fun and interesting when you don't get too serious or ambitious. Do not be discouraged by a little confusion, or your inexperience. If in doubt, just observe and learn. Take one day at a time.

INDULGENCE OR PROGRESS

38
INVOLVED

 There is a suggestion here of, not harmony exactly but, rewarding activity. It is 'the ups and downs of life' that provide your motivation, the interest, or sense of identity. You are fully occupied with the ongoing situation and have a full life. There are friendships and partnerships, or an active career, social or family life. There is a sense of belonging, or being part of something, or being involved in group activities. This is a practical time for personal and shared interests coupled with enthusiasm and material developments.

There is a lot going on around you right now, and, perhaps, you need to make sure you don't completely 'loose yourself' in the rush and confusion. If you could 'look around the corner' would you see more of the same, or something new and different ? With the energy and awareness you have, what arrives probably won't be unexpected, so it's up to you what you want.

Look to the people around you, since they always come first before any 'situation'. Deeper friendships will come when you seek others of similar interests, or extend yourself beyond your present boundaries. What you see is what you get.

CONDITIONS OR CONDITIONING

41
FAIL

You have to cope with the disappointment of failure – either personal failure, or the failure of events - and come to terms with it. This may be in your career, or personal life, and it's likely to elicit an emotional reaction or negative response that puts you off, slows you down, or stops you temporarily. You are subjected to some upsetting issues, and it's all a question of 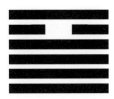 your reaction, and how this will affect your future performance and happiness, and *not* the event itself. Look out for this reaction, for you are not to take things at face value. Failure is so often seen as the opposite of success, when it may only be a chance, or change, in your life. An over-reaction with regret or resignation (defeat), nostalgia (retreat), or blame (pointless fighting after defeat), makes matters worse, and prolongs the issue.

You are a strong person who will prevail, but at the moment have been knocked by failure. If you keep a flexible inner attitude, you will regain and re-assert your power and influence later. It is this persistence with a good heart that allows you to change with the times, and find fulfilment. There is more to come. Those 'closed doors' or 'restricted' solutions, are there to stop you, or to give you something to fight against, and to involve you in the energy of failure. An actual failure, or the prospect of failure, both hold the same negative consequences. In such circumstances, failure becomes final, or a continual threat. It takes a lot of energy to fail, and to persist with failure. Let it go.

As a final resort you could let the world 'do it's worst', and find out that it's not so sure of itself after all, and in fact has no idea what it's doing. There is no reason (unless you are aware of incompetence) for your failure that chance could not have altered. Look at the facts *as they now stand*, and from this standpoint just say "Now, what's next ?" At any time you should be looking to the future, forgetting or coping with the past, and observing the present closely for introductions and offers to a new direction in your life. Let go of disappointment, it is of no use to you now, even though it may have given you some comfort in the past. This is all about a change of direction, somehow forced upon you.   Accept it, for it leads to better things.

DISAPPOINTMENT   OR   DIRECTION

42
WAIT

You seem ready to proceed with your plans but instead face a delay while the overall situation needs to develop further. You probably won't like this because it means postponing career decisions, or larger moves. The situation seems to demand a reaction, or at least worry, but keep calm. For 'uncertainty' to push you into action, would be a mistake. You do have the strength to go ahead regardless, but if you do you will face more complications and obstructions. To push ahead at this time is unwise, so you must simply wait for circumstances beyond your control to change. While you wait, relax, take some time off, and consolidate your position. This is not a standstill but a clarification of your will to succeed. The delay may well be to your advantage, or provide extra information.

At present, the situation is uncertain, but because you know what you want (and here you have the time to consider, or plan for, it), you need to be able to accept delays without worry. Conserve your energy. Do not engage in schemes that are out of your normal sphere of influence. Avoid committing yourself to any deal or offer that would obligate you at a later date. Maintain an inner optimism that things will change – then act. Accept the delay, or allow for others, or chance and change, to play their part. A lot is about to happen, and your premature interference isn't what is required right now.

Patience is a virtue. It is indeed, but in the recognition of the absence of any logic or reason to the timing of events. It is not for you to concern yourself with the timing of events. Leave it to TAO. You only have the ability to determine what you want, not when, or even where, or how. The secret of patience is to disregard the (anticipated) time element, and fulfil your plans in all other respects. Please wait, here.

DELAY   OR   DOUBT

43

SEVERANCE

There is a setback, an obstruction, or large upheaval, in your life. This could be the loss of your present lifestyle or standard of living, familiar surroundings, or relationships. There is a severance of ties. The complete severance of ties may be dramatic, or accompanied by a sense of loss or bereavement, or the potential of ruin. This is not simply another situation of  change, but the termination of a way of life or relationship. This could indicate a divorce or separation, or the loss of home or job. Your future now depends upon your capacity to acknowledge, and let go of, the past, and to seek a new life under new circumstances.

You may now see the past as 'wasted', 'precious', or 'lost', and the present as futile or meaningless, or the future as 'empty'. Reactions to past involvements, or future worries, may dominate your thinking. If you try to re-establish or re-create the past, it will mean further delay and disappointment. 'All (previous) bets are off', but you're still in the game ! If you can accept this, there is a new start in your life.

You will confront a difficult situation or face great changes. The temptation may be to make any sort of move immediately in order to show that you are still in control, or try to ignore it all, and do nothing. Unfortunately such reactions only involve you in further difficulties. A loss of drive or direction will be your greatest problem. You will need time to sort-out your life. You may need assistance or advice, before you take decisive action, or a little more time before you can plan for the future.

Now you have only to adapt to the present situation, just like everyone else, only here you cannot 'hide behind', or 'indulge in', the circumstances of your choice (like everyone else), or have the support of previous involvements. This will mean a radical new start for you, in the understanding that you remain to re-learn, re-engage, and, eventually, actually enjoy what more there is on offer. The future will offer you unseen advantages, if you let it.

RUIN   OR   RESTART

44
STAGNATION

 The circumstances or situation may seem dull, hopeless, or dead to you. While you have to depend on these circumstances, or perhaps feel trapped in the situation, you react with an angry loss of motivation, boredom, apathy, or just depression. The more you worry, the more hopeless the situation seems, until you finally give-up trying, and even then still cling-on to old habits. You tend to go along with events without much thought, and conform to circumstances that do nothing for you. There is a lack of the necessary physical or mental energy, or the resources, to progress to anything new, and hardly enough energy spare to cope with the present situation.

You need to consider your position and the relevance of what you are doing. Previously you have been going in the wrong direction, or there has been a set-back, or you have the wrong expectation. Now your mind and body is withdrawing its' support. This is often felt as a loss of appetite, vitality, 'physicality', or enthusiasm, or it can lead to a complete mental or physical breakdown. If you do nothing the situation will not improve. When faced with a number of obstacles, superior opposition, or inertia, you will 'automatically' go for a controlled withdrawal. A lack of interest could be seen as a lack of energy, but, surprisingly, this condition requires a lot of energy to sustain it, but it is energy held-in on itself. You are held-in by your thoughts and reactions, speculations and expectations, and your attitude of imprisonment. You need a release.

There is a quiet alternative. Look around you. What is the world offering you now, that you really haven't noticed, you have over-looked, or refuse to see or accept ? It is there ! The trick is to look for something quiet, ephemeral, environmental, or elemental, that has nothing to do with expectation or involvement. This could be the presence of someone, the light of day, the weather, a place. The world is fuller, gentler, and more enterprising than you allow for, but your attitude is fixed on conditions and rewards that are outmoded, and have changed, and gone. There is more on offer, and it has nothing to do with your state or abilities.

The situation around you can offer you something interesting, easy, or pleasant, to do. Take one step at a time, no matter how small it may be. Do something. Do anything ! Visit people or places. Go for a walk, or look out of the window. This action should involve physical movement whenever possible. Try a new social activity, or change your routine, or take a holiday. Do something you haven't done before. This is all about looking and listening, and being open to anything, and even the prospect of being interested. The situation is offering a way out. This new attention on what is around you will do wonders for your level of awareness, and your energy levels. There is no reason or reward here, only a casual decision to take notice of anything and everything around you.

The answer is simple, but you won't like it. Just look. Any, and even the smallest, attention leads to the greatest improvement. Even the smallest thing leads to big results. It is up to you, and how you look, not your condition, situation, or will-power. You use your considerable will-power against yourself, because there is something you cannot, or don't want to, deal with, which may well be about recognition or resentment. This problem will always demand more energy, and it will wear you down. As if contrary to all your desires and expectations, stop what you are doing, and let things be, and notice of your daily situation.
'Lightly does it' now.

APATHY OR ATTENTION

45
FEAR

 You are forced to face life, or confront a problem, but instead you face your own fear or panic. You fear the loss of independence, health, control, or security. If you've had a shock, bereavement, or accident, there may be an emotional adjustment or physical compensation going on. You could experience 'stage fright', 'panic attacks' or general insecurity. If this wasn't bad enough, you respond with stubborn or predictable behaviour, or act on emotional impulse. Your normal routine may well be disrupted, and you could make the situation worse by following that instinct towards withdrawal, or excesses in the wrong direction. You are not supposed to carry such burdens as you do, and you need to put them down for a moment, or share them with someone, in order to look at 'the facts' of your situation.

You are over-cautious, or over-compensating, for a situation that has *already* happened, or must run its' course. Your energy, although well-intentioned, adds to the problem. Don't blame others, yourself, or the situation. Your thoughts have actually nothing to do with this, but you can, and do, let them play a major role. The problem is that you have, understandably, personalised an issue or problem and made it 'emotional'. Emotions, which usually can't be controlled, and the desperate search for reasons, will not help you here. As you look at your situation, you need to apply a little compassion or a 'detached caring' to yourself. Sometimes you 'pat yourself on the back', or smile at your earnestness, and sometimes marvel at the strange turn of events. Whatever has happened, look at it as though it happened to someone else. How would you treat or advise 'this other person' ? Try a little detachment.

Perhaps an extreme solution would be to have no thoughts about anything at all, including hopes and fears, and go through life 'empty', one day at a time. If only you could do this, but that emptiness would be quickly filled, either with more thoughts to distract you, or more events and concerns to keep you involved. Actually, by seeking the emptiness (even though it isn't really possible), by *'not thinking but, instead, looking'*, you'll find that things do slow down to a pace that is right for you.

Take your own feelings, motives, fears, and your way of coping and 'avoiding', into account, but spend more time *casually looking around you*. The answer or solution is *already* there. In the present there are events, surprises, and connections, to help you get through the day. The present can provide the solution to your problems, but maybe not the whole of your past. Living in the present may be your only option, and it's one that others seek, even without the past problems.

Have some trust in your own capacity, and in the situation itself, to resolve this issue. Take things a little slower. Actually, the world and changing events may have the answer, or supply 'a way out', or friends may help. Look again.

FAITH   OR   FATE

46
WORRY

 You are being continually pulled into involvements, concerns, and enticements, and pushed into reaction, impulsive or committed (interfering) behaviour. While you remain open to all of these influences there are countless opportunities for exploitation, anxiety, and worry. You are over-involved with lots of energy to spare. If you persist on this level of activity, you can expect health problems.

When you are not fully engaged you probably feel inadequate, anxious, guilty, or just bored. You may spend a lot of time blaming others, the situation, or past events. You over-react to things that are probably nothing to do with you, or are beyond your influence or control. Your reactions are probably negative, backward looking, full of blame or guilt, or just fixed on involvement. These reactions give you 'something to do', but don't actually solve anything. You feel you must do something, but here you may have to face the fact that these problems are not going to be solved by your worry or reactions. Most of your worries are probably over things or events that you cannot control.

So, if reaction is inadvisable or ineffective, and you cannot think-up the answer, or provide a solution, you need to look elsewhere. To survive you must adopt other tactics, because if you don't, if the situation or your problems don't defeat you, your own attitude will. It's not the world that will supply what you need for happiness and fulfilment, but you ! Of course, the last place you will look for a solution is inside yourself, since you think all the gains and rewards, and the problems, are in the world.

You need a different approach, both to life, and yourself. You need to approach your situation, your daily life, and all your problems, with a different frame of mind. The trick that makes this work is that you apply this 'frame of mind' before you consider anything else. Adopt the attitude or frame of mind of "only doing what is actually in front of you". You do not need to think about anything else, although your mind, with all that energy, will tell you otherwise. Do not think about all the other issues, the consequences, or the relevance of what you are doing. Essentially this means not worrying about whether you can, or should, do anything else other than 'what is in front of you', and even whether this will have any influence at all. If you can not, or don't want to, do something right now, leave it until it actually turns-up. Tackle every aspect, task, chore, incidence, and meeting, one by one, no matter how trivial or large, to the best of your ability. You need to switch your attention on to your own action now, rather than your thoughts about it. Take each moment as it is presented to you, and quietly deal with it with no thought of the future. At first this advice will seem odd, irresponsible, or even pointless, to you.

Set your mind at ease 'inside you' first, then step out into the world. Notice that the world will continually present opportunities to you, to improve your life. It will also try to tempt you into anger, reaction, involvement, and concern for others or your future, and all those other jobs and concerns not actually present right now. 'Let the world go'. The world won't do any more to you, and *you could do a lot less to encourage it*.

Do not react, get depressed, or collapse into non-action, but instead take each day as it comes, even though others will not fail to tell you to take it more seriously than that ! Deal with each episode or task with a quiet confidence, and you will notice a real difference in the world. Your attitude, and this quiet pace, will actually change material reality for you.

You do have enough positive energy to carry this out. You also have a self-willed nature, based on mental and material expectations, which must be neutralised. You will notice the strength of your energy when you make a decision, because then, as though by chance, three or four interruptions or situations turn-up demanding your immediate attention. Deal with each one in turn, separately, and you will see that these incidences or episodes are only there to involve you, and keep you occupied, rather than to sort-out anything. With this awareness you will find that this phenomenon no longer has an effect on you. The direction you are going in, and all that rushing about, doesn't solve anything. It is an endless preoccupation obscured by guilt or worry. You, personally, can do something about your situation, but not by reacting to it, trying to alter it, or worrying about it. A change of attitude, through a change of attention, is required.

99

You should consider what it is you want out of life before you get diverted by all those other problems, and everyone else's views. Your own direction in life, and use of your energies, may well be just to take it easy, and enjoy yourself, and everything else is a bonus, a passion, or a delight. Stand to one side and let everything proceed without you. This will give you a clearer picture of what is actually going on, and the inner space to sort out your own interests and enjoyments.

If you are good at this, instead of just going through the motions, you will add humour, enthusiasm, and generosity, *just when you thought it's the last thing you need, or could provide.* Go on, surprise yourself !

REACTION OR RELAXATION

47

REGULATION

It is not regulation and control that you need, but gratification. The issue here is an inner one of attitude, self-esteem, or motivation. You are dissatisfied in some way, or seek approval, motivation, or meaning, but tend to over-indulge or over-restrict yourself as a sort of compensation. You feel you need to start, but cannot 'get around to it'. This leads to periods of strict 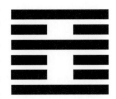 discipline, or fierce regimes of denial. There is an inner desire for physical, sensual, or material, expression or appreciation, but you are stopped by yourself, or the situation you are in. You are, basically, discontented with the present, and may spend a lot of time looking at the dissatisfaction in your life. However, that concern, regret, disapproval, or resentment, is in *your heart*, not the world, or others, even though you seek the solution there.

The answer is simple, although to you it won't appear to address the problem. You only need come to terms with your own needs and desires, and the level of comfort that is right for you, before you try and alter yourself and the world. A balance is needed between what you want out of life and how you intend to get it 'comfortably'. If you react to that word 'comfortable' you know you have a problem. 'Moderation in many things' would be a wise ambition.

Your position is not hopelessly confined to your present state. You can change, improve, or develop, but you need to do it at a much slower pace than you would like. It is this prospect of 'delay' that puts you off, or diverts you into all sorts of schemes, promises, and regrets. Avoid the inclination to completely change yourself immediately, otherwise you will end up confused or diverted.

To impose regulation on yourself, or others, will meet with resistance and opposition. If regulation causes tension it is likely to be counter-productive. In normal circumstances regulation is a means to an end, not the end itself. In your case the regulation has taken-over, and there is a continual demand for improvement. Dissatisfaction, addictions, or indulgence, keep you busy, for without them you are lost. If you think you can solve your problems with regulation or abortive discipline, you merely change the manner of the problem, not find a solution. The consequences are that you can become involved in an endless pursuit of gratification and its denial. It is endless, and hopeless, and until you can see this, you are trapped. The sign that this energy flow is 'not working' (although it does precisely what it's programmed to do), is the lack of lasting results, lots of set-backs, and the need for more effort. *Actions or pursuits reflect inner states of mind,* NOT improve them or change them.

You need to change, not your body, or your mind, or your appearance, or the rest of the world. You need to change the *direction of your energy*. You can see this in your attitude or approach. You choose physical means, say exercise, eating habits, or how you look, when you should consider a mental, inner, change of attitude. You could choose intellectual or idealistic interests, or entertainments, an educational or personal attainment or project, or an 'impossible dream'. Alternatively, you choose mental depression, apathy, or loss of energy or enthusiasm, when you actually need a more physical approach. Go for a walk, visit people or places, try sport or go to the gym, and cut down watching TV. 'Get out and about'. You have lost sight of the fact that *each day* has a different 'edge' or 'feel', or weather, or prospect. The world is a material and physical place, and so are you. The prospects are endless, and changeable.

Perhaps you, rightly, blame others, or the situation, for your continued unhappiness, but they are not listening. Look to yourself, but now consider an inner change of attitude. You cannot 'try to do this', for it comes from an understanding of how involved or concerned you are. It is your own heart and mind you deal with, not anyone else's. Accept and let go of others, and the situation, and it will let go of you. This detachment allows you to go your own way, regardless of others. No one will stop you doing what you want to do.

Decide without excuses or reasons, guilt or blame, what you really want to do, or where you really want to be. If you have no idea, this is part of your problem, with its' attendant gratifications to 'fill the gap'. Seek interests – physical, mental, or spiritual, but not, at this stage, emotional. You can realise your own dream, because it inspires you, regardless of anyone else. Even the impossible can be achieved, one way or another, when you know what you want. Take each step easily, quietly, and comfortably.

DISSATISFACTION OR DISCOVERY

48

ADJUST

Your notions are wrong, or you face a situation that is 'closed' or 'fixed'. Now would be a good time to 'sort yourself out', with an adjustment of your expectations, and priorities. Unfortunately, there is in your character or attitude an unwillingness to take advice, accept change, or face personal criticism, because your notions and attitudes hold you up. That  is, they give you something to strive for, while they also stop any further development.

There are too many expectations and demands. Your aspirations and 'high hopes' may require more material resources than you have, or you are working too hard to attain perfection. You need to take note of the actual conditions, relationships, and circumstances, around you, as opposed to your own assumptions and expectations, which often stand in the way of any change, either in yourself or your situation. It is so often easier, and more satisfying, to blame others or the situation, and to battle 'against the odds'. There will always be something wrong, so that Inflowing Energy can feed on itself endlessly. This is your problem, and you will live with it, or change.

There is a sense of conflict within you, or about your purpose or intentions, or with your status or position. Unfortunately you don't want to hear this. Your ego, obsession, or over-confidence, could be a problem, so you need to be careful in your attitude, approach, or judgements. In any event, avoid legal battles. The object here should be to secure your own comfort and happiness, not take-on, or blame, the rest of the world for your lack of status.

Your ambition to achieve the status and satisfaction you desire, only further isolates you. Consider the direction you are taking, and how this should reflect your future objectives. Deal with the real world with what you have to offer, not what you think it with-holds from you. You need to be capable and relaxed, rather than assertive and forceful. As it now stands, you are competing with yourself, through the world and others, and will face endless problems. Accept your present situation for what it is, and improve it with what you have now.

EXPECTATIONS   OR   DEMANDS

51
ACCESS

 You have access to a new situation, or are introduced to someone or something, that changes the course of your life. There are new enterprises, new people, and new locations. This may be an engagement, a new job, or a commitment to self-development or education. Consider realistic goals, or a new start. Travel is indicated, or the need to travel may be the first sign of change. This is a big step towards the realisation of your plans, or at least the foundation to a potential that you may not be fully unaware of. This is the start of a new phase in your life.

A whole new life is offered, but you may feel some natural hesitation, or doubt, about the direction this presents. You need nothing more than enthusiasm. The trick is to be friendly. There's plenty out there in the world, and only denial stops you. Just say "Yes" to everything new and unknown, for you certainly have the strength and drive to see it through. It's time to go for it.

OPTION AND OPTIMISM

52

ISOLATION

You find yourself in awkward conditions in a social, work, family, or a group situation, in which you must be careful. There may be a period of, possibly enforced, separation from loved ones or familiar surroundings. You may accept this as part of your plans, or as necessary, or it may be the result of certain circumstances that you will be aware of. You are, in  some sense, 'on your own', but that doesn't mean you cannot find help or comfort from others. Basically, you are at odds with your circumstances or situation.

You are either too sensitive, or too thoughtful, or too cultured, to cope with existing conditions. The world is wrong, not you. Some people will flourish now and seek to exploit the situation even further, but do not be moved to reaction by events in the world, or the actions of others. Avoid the temptation to try and influence others, avoid unpleasant people, and don't become part of the noise and confusion.

Material or physical opposition or reaction on your part is useless. You are drawn into solitary activity in order to cope, or sort things out. You need an inner, creative, response in order to maintain your own enthusiasm and integrity. You have to maintain this inner adaptability and sensitivity, whilst not showing it outwardly. In this way you achieve a balance between yourself and the, perhaps oppressive, nature of your circumstances.

In times such as these, your best option is to stand well back. This places you in a more favourable position to act when this regime ends, as it will. This situation is only temporary, but the mistake or danger would be to accept its' apparent stability as permanent, and loose your chance of freedom because you have given-up, or remain committed to opposition, or some past conditions. Things change.

Go cautiously and quietly for the time being, and maintain your inner resolve. A sense of optimism, and a little humour, and an occasional shared response, will see you through.

APART   AND   ADAPT

105

53
OBSERVE

 Chance and change enter your life. There are a number of opportunities, introductions, or invitations, presented to you, sometimes in a disguised form, or in the most unlikely of circumstances. There are unexpected changes to your plans which benefit you later in some way. At times such as these, you should look about you, not just in a receptive or sensitive way, but with enthusiasm, for the potential around you, believe it or not, is vast.

You are surrounded by a great source of information. Use it to your advantage. What you know, see, or suspect, is true. By simply observing actions and words out of context you can see the true nature of people. If you actually trust your intuition, optimism, or sense of judgement, things will go very well for you.

Your attitude conditions, and forms, what you see. Your own thinking not only changes your perception, but how things turn out. You'll get what you expect. Simply observe what you are given with a little detachment, and you will see the way forward.

SURPRIZE !   SMILE !

54
CONCERN

You are constrained in some way by your circumstances, or feel unstable or unsure about yourself or your situation, or feel unable to cope. You face circumstances which prevent you from enjoying life to the full, or cause you concern, doubt, worry, and stress. When you push forward you only find yourself up against greater problems. The less you do, the
more hopeless you feel. If you react to this with self-pity, a negative attitude, or resentment, you can make the situation a lot worse. The reason for all this trouble is your own action and reaction. You could of course blame the situation or those around you, but it is really about you, and *what you want to do*.

Some might say that you must resign yourself to adversity, but you, particularly, must not match negative events or situations with negative feelings. Such a combination, with the strength you have, will have disastrous consequences. You will just double your trouble. No, do not try harder. No, do not give up. No, do not retreat, or blame your circumstances. You only need to stop reacting. All of your activity and involvement is designed to divert or distract you, by fixing your attention *on anything other than what you want out of life*.

It appears that you are continually on the brink of disorder or disaster. Worry, fear, and uncertainty, giving you the notion that you are unable to cope, are all inner emotional states, even when based on, or put on, external events. Whatever the cause of the problems, or how real or upsetting they are, the more you react to them, the more problems you will face. An insight into all of this should prompt you to realise that further physical or material reaction is useless. There is nothing you can do about your situation, except change your attitude. Perhaps, you still think you have a fighting chance, or that you have not yet reached the end, so this is one piece of advice you certainly won't like, even though you possess the power to implement it. "Smile ! and the world will change with you." Ironically, the *more* you reject this 'nonsense' advice, the stronger its' effect when you do give it a go.

You have been committed to fighting and reacting, and feel that you can't change now for that would look like failure, giving-up, or a denial of your experience, or admitting that more effort won't work. Unfortunately, the world out there doesn't give a damn how you feel, or what you are committed to, or whether you are a success or a failure. Of course, your emotion and struggle won't just go away since they are based on deep patterns of thought, behaviour, and responsibility.

Learning to cope is *only a matter of satisfying 'just yourself' first*. Thinking and acting for others, however necessary or admirable, will only work if you can do it 'easily'. If effort, concern, guilt or approval, are present you will either exhaust yourself, or expose yourself to unending pressure. Stability starts inside you, *not* in the world, and, in this sense, the world, and those other people, will never give you 'an even break', or release you from your duties and responsibilities. Only you can do that.

So, from now on approach the world in a very shallow way, as it will seem to you. It sounds odd, but you need to treat all events and situations with the impersonal respect they deserve. Sort things out as a series of 'impersonal' tasks. Avoid, and make excuses for, some tasks, as it suits you not others. Don't get emotionally involved. Apart from all the upheavals and real problems you face, the real issue here is your own confidence and happiness. A quiet satisfaction is your aim, but this is something that you will have to aim for, not just wait for it to turn-up. You, particularly, have to avoid the conclusion that things will always be the same, but the reactions and the involvements will continue until you 'settle-down' in yourself. Develop, encourage, and even act-out, optimism, interest and enthusiasm, whenever you can. *Just for yourself.* Act in a carefree way, as though things are improving. If you cannot do any of this, just 'ease up' in your thinking and feeling about things, and others, and watch the difference this makes.

This positive energy, so unconnected to 'reality', will save you, even though it will appear to you to be going in the wrong direction. Gain some pleasure or enjoyment from something every day, no matter how small. Look about you and change only the smallest of details or concerns. Let the 'big stuff' sort itself out. Most of the time it is enough just to take one day at a time. Listen to others, and smile. Be adaptable and, when you get the chance, spontaneous. Change the focus, or place, of your attention.

It is the expressions of optimism, humour, acceptance, love, interest and enthusiasm, that protect you from all that involvement in life's problems. It is your attitude or awareness, not the world, that makes things happen. It's so easy to distract you !, but also, if you ever wished to pursue it, to delight you ! If you have no plan, or, more importantly, no effective method to enjoy yourself and make yourself comfortable, all the chances and changes in life will merely confuse or defeat you.

Develop a 'lighter' approach, by not taking things and others *quite so seriously*. This lesson, if learnt, will provide you with a personal stability far superior to anything else in life, which will sustain you beyond the present time. It is a lesson taught, often in the most difficult conditions, and consequently seldom learnt.

DISTRACTION   OR   DELIGHT

55

PROMOTION

 There will be a recognition of the work you have done, or a reward for your past efforts or persistence. There is a breakthrough or release, or a promotion in career matters or social standing. When you know what you want, and have done all in your power to secure it, expect promotion. That next step may not be entirely as you planned, but your ambitions are going to be realised. Most of the work has been done. Consolidate your position and maintain a sense of confidence and ease. Don't be overly concerned about the 'how', or 'when', of promotion.

Pay a little attention to your image, because it's all about who you know, or you being in a position to be seen. Have another look at those areas you consider least important, and complete all tasks in hand before you move on. Get rid of the clutter of the past. Get yourself ready now. Don't be afraid to aim for the top.

PREPARATION OR RELEASE

56
INTERFERANCE

You face a number of obstructions that have evolved through your daily situation, and you feel threatened, offended, or dissatisfied by the development of events, and yet you still push ahead. The obstructions may arise from the situation itself, from inner insecurities, or your own stubborn behaviour, and if you think about it, these 'problems' may have been with  you for a long time. You feel as if you have heavy commitments and responsibilities, or you mistrust others' abilities, or you may have a pessimistic outlook or attitude. All of this leads you into an over-protective or over-defensive state. All of this will make you suspicious of, or discontented with, the progress of events. You are inclined to interfere, no doubt for the best reasons, because it is 'standards' or some future state or condition that you feel the need to control. Everyone finds their own level. You either haven't found yours, or it's rather negative, or you wish to impress it upon everyone else.

Usually the best way to deal with obstructions is to walk around them, or approach them from a position of compromise to sort out the problem, or to act with support and co-operation. One would only confront an obstruction head-on if one had no choice, no self control, or exercised too much control. Such is the case here. You feel the need to meet an obstruction head-on and face the consequences, perhaps because of your sense of duty. While you remain like this the effect is of an irresistible force meeting an immovable object. Here is a warning that your present approach will end in disaster. You cannot win, even if you refuse to admit defeat. You continue to impose your view, react, or interfere, but this merely changes the nature of the problems, not remove them.

There is a possibility that your attitude, standards, or objectives, may be inappropriate for others. The deeper you get involved, the more you project your faults and fears onto others and the situation. Your response makes matters worse, possibly causes the problem, and certainly fuels it. There are always, at least, two sides to a problem – and you may be one of them. The result is either obsessive interference, resentment, or emotional exhaustion.

You do have the ability to sort things out, but you must exercise some caution and self-control. It's time to relax your high standards, and *become a little more at ease with your surroundings*. There is a deeper issue here in your personal frustration, or your inability to enjoy yourself, or, at least, be comfortable. Look at the present situation in a detached fashion, and consider exactly what all your efforts hope to achieve. Look at your views and ambitions, and compare them with the world. You only need to adapt and adjust your plans and views, to make your life a little more comfortable and interesting. You could be quiet for once, take a holiday, or let the rest of the world operate at its' own speed. Whatever the problems, you need to change your level of involvement, stand back a bit, and let things be.

Don't take it all *so seriously !*

ACCEPT   OR   ADJUST

57
DUTY

A family matter needs your care or attention. Familiarity, responsibility, or restrictions, are highlighted. A discussion, consideration, or action, is required. With some material benefits and status comes an obligation that extends beyond merely personal desires. Your duty or responsibility is defined by others, which you may accept, exploit, or feel exploited by it.
Social or family responsibility and strength are indicated here, but there may be some problems. Even in a shared atmosphere there is bound to be a 'battle of wills'. When you are flexible in your responses you will prosper.

You have a duty to maintain order and allow for personal expression, but neither must be at the cost of the future happiness and progress, of those concerned. Uncontrolled, selfish, or unreasonable, behaviour must always be tackled, even if it causes temporary distress. If you have to compromise, consider the nature and desire of what is asked for, and, by using subtlety, always seek the future or long term advantage.

Your duty is clearly defined by existing relationships, which can only be maintained by loyalty and acceptance. Your circumstances should reflect happiness and sharing, not simply provide conditions or conditioning. If you cannot do your duty with a good heart, and if responsibility and desire do not co-exist, you'll have to sort-out your priorities or discuss your situation. Families grow, or repeat.

RESTRICTION OR RESPONSIBILITY

58
GROWTH

 Something beyond your present awareness is going on, which needs your attention. There are creative, personal, spiritual, or psychic, avenues open to you. You should seek-out others of a like-mind, and need information, or contact with others, to grow, learn, and practice. This is a time of inner development, and finding your own particular way of working, perhaps as a specialist in your field, since there is a career option open to you. With your talent, 'you can go anywhere, do anything, if you're not in a hurry'.

It may well be that you possess some degree of natural psychic ability. This means that you could have a talent as either a Medium ['talking to dead people', or communicating with 'spirits'], a Clairvoyant [seeing the future, possibly through card reading, etc.], or you may be a 'Sensitive' [in the use of a sixth sense] that allows you to sense or feel things in an unusual way. The use of a device, or method, may enable you to assess, find, or change, things or people, as in dowsing, or using a pendulum, or 'healing', etc. You may have a 'knowing' or wisdom, which you can use to advise others, often beyond your own personal experience. At first this is a strong intuition, or even sense of rightness, and if you trust it, it can develop into 'messages', then guidance.

You do have one, or more, of these talents. Go on your own interests and intuition. With the use of your imagination, intuition, and sensitivities, you will 'see', know, or 'feel', extra information that can be practically applied to others or the situation. Your imagination is your link with *The Otherside* (the land of dreams, dreamers, symbols, and spiritual forces). You can use your imagination as a way, a language, or tool, to enquire, to change, and to improve. It is that part of your imagination that is not personal or emotional that is 'the place that you can enter'. In this 'state' your imagination and your intuition are 'real', and form and inform 'reality', as a flow of energy.

With this kind of energy, remember to 'play at it'. Being 'serious', thinking too much, or seeking reasons or proof, can totally stop the flow. There is an 'impersonal', detached, 'full', quality to all of this that you can also sense in normal reality as 'a resonance', (a sort of balance/feeling/ 'glow').

All of this can be subverted by the ego, dogma, and systems that seek to explain, possess, and promote. The ego, with social and personal status, are the closed doors to any increased spiritual awareness. Conventional standards, attitudes, or beliefs, will hinder your inner development.

You can now put natural, spontaneous, and sometimes unusual, abilities into action. New ideas may be introduced, personal confidence developed, and greater freedom enjoyed. Trust and use your imagination and intuition now. Make plenty of room in your life for the unexpected, and 'unexplainable'.

INSIGHT OR IMAGINATION

61
WORK

 You have a tendency to be overly caught-up or involved in the daily events of life. The ambitions of career, commonplace duties, or the needs and necessities of family life, all make demands on your time. The more involved you get, the fuller your life apparently becomes. The indications are that you can get too involved in matters, to the point that there is no room for anything else.

Being single-minded produces results and can lead to great rewards, but it can also be a form of self-distraction or obsession. This points to a person who is busy 'for its' own sake'. Busyness, or business, may be your way of coping, and to you "effort = reward". Unfortunately, with this formula, if you ever get the balance wrong, or if there is any delay, you will certainly know about it through stress, frustration, exhaustion, or failure.

The world is a busy place, and you tend to be busy too. Even though this may be interesting and involving, what stands in the way of harmony is your inclination to over-do it, or be in too much of a hurry at times. To be serious about fulfilling all your duties and responsibilities, and interests, you have to be organised, and have some 'free-time'. Your timetable must include you, not exclude you. You could relieve the tension, and re-charge your batteries, by taking time off to enjoy yourself and your *present* surroundings, for no other reason, and at no extra cost.

You have an over-active mind, sense of duty, or emotional involvement. There will always be just one more thing to attend to, or one last problem to solve. Once you realise this, you will see that it is endless, and that a lot of energy is being expended. While this suits you, there will be no apparent problem, but 'the world' has a tendency to leave behind those who don't 'keep up the pressure'.

The relationship you have with the world, work, with family and others, depends on you and your interests, comfort, and well-being, not all the other factors. Even though family, ambition, status, purpose or pleasure, are important, you come first. That distinction, and that awareness of an inner sensibility, may have eluded you.

DISTRACTED OR FOCUSED

62
LEAD

It's time you took responsibility for your own life, and your relationship to others. "Relationships" are not your responsibility, but your choice. You can change the world you live in, in a practical way to suit yourself, and others. When you do not act or make decisions, others will, with probably less satisfying results. In most cases, the only thing stopping you  taking-on responsibility, and the rewards, is your own hesitation, laziness, or distraction over the details. Prioritise now, be selective, and make choices. It is time to lead your own life under your own terms.

On another level, people may 'look up to you', and you may lead, or be asked to lead, a group, a family, or take charge in an enterprise. This places you in a special position, with greater responsibilities. You need to be aware of the motivations and aspirations of others, and be able to adapt the aims of your 'group' to almost any circumstances.

You do have the ability to exploit and manipulate others, to get the best out of them and the situation. These manipulative qualities should be coupled with motivation and authority, but, actually, what is really required is enthusiasm, and it's sensitive or adaptable application. Listen to others. Listen to the situation. Leadership will take-up a lot of your time, so it is essential that you not only become the expert, but enjoy what you do.

For some, on a personal level, it may now be the time to go out and meet people and do more things, and embrace the busy world. Actually, no one will expect anything from of you, and you could always do far less, or nothing, but it's time to 'come out of hiding'. You need to do this in a relaxed and easy fashion, with no other motive than to interest or enjoy yourself. If you are out of practice, or shy, at first engage people, total strangers and acquaintances, *for only two or three minutes at a time*. Be casual, take an interest, and give them your total undivided attention, and smile. Visit people or places, or pursue any activity, *for less than twenty minutes*, then move on. Small steps. Huge results, with more to come. No one else will mention it, and maybe disagree or disapprove, but, for you, the world out there, with all its' people and places, is your playground !

RESPONSIBILITIES AND REWARDS

63

ORGANISE

There are changes and opportunities, and a sense of direction. To go forward you will need a plan or objective, in life or in business. Practical and material issues are now very important, and you can achieve something in educational, career, or property matters. There is a potential for progress, and in this progressive phase things must be organised. Pay attention to the details, and arrange the information to promote your cause.

In business the objective is to make money, not spend it, and yet the greater the investment, the greater the potential profit. Ambition and desire must be regulated by *present* resources. To calculate on future profits and resources is not so much organisation, but chance.

Two distinct philosophies and approaches emerge in "Effort = Reward", and "Enjoy Now". You do have a choice, and all the facts can be re-presented to suit your case. You could be comfortable and enjoy life, or be fulfilled in some way, or 'work at it' for some future reward. A simple assessment of your priorities, your desires and hopes, and your actual daily life or routine, will establish your level here. Often it is a choice between present comfort and satisfaction, or desire and future status. Either way can be achieved through organisation, in a practical and measured approach to the world. Once established, it needs to be adaptable, sometimes spontaneous, and always centred on the main objective.

If you are uncertain about any existing organisation or situation (or indeed, any person), look at the actual activities of the leader, or centre, and also the outer fringes, regardless of supposed aims or ideals. That will tell you what is actually going on. In much the same way, you could look at your own life and ask if all the progress and organisation is actually producing the results you want.

DETAILS OR DATES

64
CONTROL

A time of progress and development, but you need to relax your high standards, competitive ambition, or desire for complete control over the situation. There may be an element of insecurity and worry, so you need to become a little more at ease with your surroundings. The resolution of your problems or finances is under your control, but not, as it were, in your 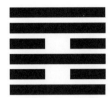 control. You may be over-involved or over-committed. You can achieve what you want, but the wise management of your resources requires an overview and detachment. There is no need to be aggressive, or to worry about the future. Actually, people will go along with you if you give them plenty of room. By relaxing your obstinate hold on matters material and mental, you will find that the problems sort themselves out. You should be optimistic.

The solution to whatever problems you might face lies in your own quiet persistence. There is, however, an element of stress in your approach, which you need to address. Despite any competition or obstructions, you need to work, with yourself and others, in a spirit of subtle compromise. Somewhat paradoxically, you need to take it easy. This is not a sign of weakness, but of confidence.

If you can accept things and people as they are, perhaps against your better judgement, you will reduce your need to alter and control things. If you can do this, you will find that the world does proceed efficiently enough, without your concern. To control your strength it must be used in subtle, easy, or unseen, ways, and not simply to demonstrate or enforce your position. Let go of all those outdated projects. You don't need them to be who you are. Let go of concerns, especially if they do not directly concern you. Avoid confrontation and reaction. The world is here to accommodate you, but it could also provide endless 'self-appointed' stress and strain. TAO runs itself. You are only here for the ride. There is no hurry. Events will lead you at this time. Your strength will be lost if you try to control too much and too soon. Adapt lightly, and you'll succeed.

RELAX OR HOLD

65

AUTHORITY

 A strong-minded person, or authority figure, or a social situation, perhaps in the form of a demanding job, or a restrictive family situation, exerts some control over your life. Things are organised in such a way that you can only make minor adjustments (if any). Someone else is in charge. What you face is larger or stronger than you, and you may accept this for the protection, security, or assurance, it gives you. The most you can hope for in these circumstances is a modest satisfaction in what you do. Even so, there is interference from others.

You are probably dealing with an individual or situation that is fixed or set in its' ways, and are attempting to introduce a lighter, or different, approach. As things now stand, you don't have much chance of success. If you attempt more than minor changes, in the belief that the balance of power should be equal, or that you have a greater influence, then you will invite a reaction, or reprisals, or possibly mental or physical abuse. By subtle means, you may be able to change things a little by employing a sympathetic nature, humour, pleasant social manners, and disarming openness. This is done without causing a reaction, when you pose no threat. Such is your situation.

If your freedom of choice is restricted by those who have other, and even your own, interests at heart, you can be sure it's time for a change. You may be in a position where you are not expected to exert any influence at all, and can please yourself what you do. If this simple freedom is also denied you, you must seriously consider your position. Your integrity, whether you support or oppose the status-quo, is fundamental to any future developments. You have enough 'self-will', or confidence, not to accept this situation as matter of convention or circumstance, and there is the option of trying to change the situation, but change, as such, is unlikely, for here it is all a question of balance. The balance that presently exists may give you more than you loose, or you may plan to change your situation radically, and face the prospect of loosing what you already have. Your choice is between wise interdependence and accepting subordination, or a complete change, and start again. Only by being aware of the 'limitations' or boundaries of your situation can you hope to succeed. This does place you in a position to upset things, an individual, or the situation generally, by your behaviour. There is a possibility that you may be in the wrong place at the moment, or may be insufficiently prepared for anything else.

Of course, there is one fact that you have overlooked, and that is, whatever happens, you can always rely on you. If you are true to your nature you will get the balance right, and decide when, or if, change is necessary. Are you optimistic, far-sighted, satisfied, or simply resigned to your situation ? You decide.

Your horizons are viewed from here.

INTERFERANCE OR INFLUENCE

66
PROGRESS

All things change in time, but sometimes it doesn't seem quick enough. Slow progress can simply be the natural timing of events, or the result of a cautious attitude, or a methodical approach. Either way, at this point in time, this is probably the correct pace for you. Slow progress does have a strengthening quality to it, absent perhaps in sudden change and rapid advancement. You have the energy and capacity to organise most material matters, but present conditions dictate the speed and course of events. The tasks you now complete determine the quality of later successes. When the time is right, the next step will improve your image and your prospects.

Use this time now to set firm foundations for the future, and pay attention to the practical details. You do well to remain in the practical sphere to which you are committed, and there is nothing wrong with you or your abilities, which may involve quality or craftsmanship. Your progress may even appear dull or lacklustre to some, who seem to go faster or have more. You need to continue as you are doing for this allows for progressive changes, inner development, and experience, at the same time.

At the start things are slow, and you may be without companionship, but with progress comes support and a secure base from which to proceed with confidence. There will be a materially successful partnership or marriage. Slow progress endures, and is a strength not a weakness. Satisfaction is the name of the game, and you will get there.

PURPOSE OR PRACTICE

67
BEGIN

You are going to start a totally new direction in your life in, possibly, uncertain conditions. With motivation and enthusiasm you will be able to overcome any obstacles or barriers in your way. The barriers are there to deter others who are not quite ready, but for you this is the start of a new enterprise or phase in your life, which may involve a lengthy  undertaking. Remember, you are selected because you have the capacity to develop, and that development rests *not* upon the trials and tests you may face, but on your attitude of acceptance and enthusiasm.

The key to your progress at this stage is receptiveness and trust, and enthusiasm which will later develop into ambition. There are social and personal introductions which lead to lasting friendships or relationships. You can expect changes in your daily routine and responsibilities, and possibly in your personal appearance. Be prepared to change as much as the situation around you, and develop new skills and friendships. There may be a change of heart, a rebirth or birth, which leads to long term relationships and commitments.

Your progress will not be blocked, so act with enthusiasm. You may need to walk around some obstacles, try another direction, adapt, or reconsider expectations. If you are uncertain, stop and think, or seek advice. Smile, and talk to someone. Just listen, and you will be offered a solution. Above all, accept it, go easy on yourself, and just 'go with the flow' for now.

TRUST   OR   TRY

TAO I CHING

68
INFLUENCE

 This is the time to start, or complete, a plan, project, or scheme. The introduction of a new spirit or idea can lead to great changes. You have the chance to make your influence felt. You have a talent, skill, or creative approach, that will have an influence over others. Consider professional or commercial outlets for your talents. There is the distinct possibility that your idea, concept, or inspiration, will influence and change peoples' lives, or, at least, be successful and financially rewarding.

There are two directions. One could be in the form of wisdom, words, writing, or philosophy and attitude, which will require 'productive solitude'. Before you start, you'll need to get your 'own story' in order first. You have a lot to offer, and it's time to "be published or damned". Write, diversify, teach !

The other direction is through a creative approach. Think in terms of your own ideas, optimism and enthusiasm, and how you can integrate these into any job or project. You will amaze, amuse, or attract, to engage the enthusiasm and confidence of others. This will need experience or resources before it can be successful.

Do not rush into things. Pace yourself, for all of this can take a little time. For some this may mean 'a late start in life', but time has got nothing to do with 'the right moment'. Expect the improbable. Do the impossible.

PLAN OR PRODUCE

71
CONFIDENCE

You express your abilities and talents to the full. You have passion, ambition, conviction, and prejudice. You proceed regardless, based on your strength and status, and ego. From this there is an increase in material benefits and possessions, which leads naturally to personal progress, unless of course you over-indulge or over-extend yourself. Favourable  circumstances are not always enough to ensure good fortune, for confidence can develop into egotism. Beware of your own convictions, of impulsive, but controlled, action, for if you ever proceed on your own status or ability, without first looking at the situation, or even monitoring the consequences, you can expect eventual failure. Chance and change rule, not you.

Let your ambitions and actions be guided by an unhurried confidence. Confidence is not shown in strength, but ease. You can inspire others with your sense of ease and enthusiasm, and your conviction. Providing you are convinced, others will follow. It must be said that this 'conviction' may be an act on your part, but provided you feel it, others will respond.

At this time you will achieve, or get close to, your ambitions, and have influence and power. Progress does not stop there, but continues in the diligent management of your resources. Consolidate as well as diversify. Go for it !, but look before you leap, with power.

CONVICTION OR CHANCE

72
ACCEPT

 This is the time for you to come to terms with your circumstances, and to accept the facts of the situation, at whatever age or state you may be in. It's like stepping off a treadmill for a moment to look at what is going on around you, and within you. Stop for a moment, even while everything else keeps on going. You've arrived !, but it probably isn't what you expected, at your age, sex, occupation, or location.

You may have been saving the notion that you've arrived until you reached completion, perfection, or security. This notion however is a mental one, and could be applied at any time. When you've arrived, it's O.K. to slow down, for you still have time to achieve your ambitions. It is a time to assess your situation, and those ambitions may need to be scaled down, or up, but no great change will happen until you accept that you are here, now. If you resent, or do not accept, your place in the world or the situation you are in now, you will face continual interference or uncertainty.

Do not make comparisons with others, or speculate on the future, or the past. Some say that this is a particular 'time of life' crisis or conclusion, but it could happen at any time. You are the product of your circumstances, but if you react to this at face value, you will be directly affected by all sorts of constraints and considerations. Reaction, regret, resignation or nostalgia, are time and energy consuming, and only hold you back. Your response is half, or the whole, of the problem, and the solution. You may be looking at the world through the eyes of others, or may have taken-on attitudes, standards, and expectations, that don't actually reflect your own situation and needs. You could go right back to the beginning of your childhood to find your true nature, and only then see how the world has imposed its' view, and how you've coped with that. Either way, you are here now, in this situation, and you may be inclined to use status, and particularly the status of others, as a measure of success.

It is the time to move on to the next phase of your life, but you will not do this if you first have to sort-out, compensate for, or condemn, all that has gone on in the past. You just need to forget it ! Such an attitude may seem irresponsible to you, but it is the only way you can develop, with the energy and nature that you have.

An attitude of acceptance and trust, and a little optimism, will see you through any situation, but you must change with the times. Even so, sometimes the world can present obstructions that apparently cannot be passed. This may be due to personal misfortune, social controls, or simply the way things turn-out. Perhaps your standards and beliefs, or cherished notions and desires, are questioned or unlikely to be achieved. At times such as these you may not be able to depend on others, fate, or familiar solutions. How you resolve this very much depends on how you relate and adapt, which might be easier than you think.

To accept your situation and circumstances now, without any more emotional thinking, will allow you to direct your attention and energies to a daily improvement of your situation. Look at the essentials, of comfort, well-being, and interest, rather than the desire for more, or change. It's a strange way to look at things, perhaps, but you are not actually going anywhere. You are here now, and it's not so bad when you make yourself comfortable. That's all you can do, and it's more than enough.

By all means maintain and revise your plans, but keep a close eye on the present. The present moment will sustain you, and you will find that your body and mind are pretty good indicators of what is right for you after all, if only you listened. This could be a turning point in your life. Independence of Spirit is on offer.

ARRIVAL   OR   DEPARTURE

73
RESPONSE

 The world, your situation, certain individuals, or even your own intuition, will be offering you avenues of progress. Your response to unexpected or unlikely opportunities, or apparently unpromising associations, will determine the future course of your life. These chances may not be obvious at first, or may seem to have little potential, but all that is required is your response and active participation. In other words, be clever enough to see and accept things as they are happening, rather than wait for something else.

TAO can work exceedingly swift, or be very slow because you never asked, or it may reflect your continued delay, disapproval, or desires. It seems you get what you ask for, what you expect, or what you allow yourself. In this respect, whatever is presented to you has the potential, no matter how unlikely it looks, to work to your advantage if you allow it to. It is like a sort of permission to take what is on offer and improve it, not continually wait for perfection. You give yourself that permission with your attitude, and it has nothing to do with conditions in the world, status, or finances. This could be a turning point in your life if an option is taken.

Respond with your heart, which may sometimes be unconnected to reason, or your responsibilities. Listen to your inner desires or knowing', not your experience. What is offered here may be more than an opportunity. It may be the start, or confirmation, of a more open approach. Without the responsibility of following your experience, which is a memory set into attitude, you may be open to a more spontaneous approach to the world and what it offers.

If you have some degree of originality this must not be sacrificed to convention or conformity, but adapted to the direction you take in your life. Use your enthusiasm, and your imagination, for your own advantage, not just everyone else's. Make a list or plan of what you want in life, which will include possessions and passions. 'How' you ask, is what you get, so be optimistic, and you will be open to the possibility of getting what you want.

ASK OR REPLY

74
CONFLICT

There are opportunities for progress, but you conflict in some way with the situation, or with others. Rights, standards, or status, come into question, and justification, jealousy, or blame, may arise. This is due to your attitude, motivations, or your behaviour. This lack of trust could become very negative. You just won't let go. The warning signs are resentment, regret, nostalgia, envy, and struggle. This you may accept as necessary without wishing to change, for it stems from your position, your ambition, or emotional problems based on past experiences. It may be because of past emotional abuse or physical violence that you feel the need to re-assert, or retaliate against, the situation, and want to gain more control. This means a lack of trust or generosity, and usually points to an unnecessary victim, or a bully.

A strong personal ambition lies behind an apparent amiability. You thrive on competition, even to the point of open conflict. It seems you use a considerable amount of energy to overcome obstacles. Unfortunately these are more to do with your own inner insecurities or past problems, than actual conditions. If you are not careful, you will find that the harder you try, or the more you want, the greater the problems become.

Here is someone looking for a fight !, and the world provides enough opponents. To remain in the game you must be flexible, and avoid opponents (situations, people, or systems) that have a greater, or opposite, strength. While your strength and attention is applied on, or against, others or the situation, you will have conflict.

The answer lies in a different direction. You may be surprised to find that, with the energy you have, you may be more at ease with your circumstances than you realised, or have allowed for. Make yourself comfortable with what you already have.

REVENGE OR REFORM

75

RESTRAINT

 You feel the need to push ahead, to organise, or control the situation, but are apparently stopped by others, or events. Whatever the reasons you can supply, it is you who is not ready, although this observation may seem unfair to you. There is a delay, a complication, or an obstruction. This may highlight a sense of conflict within you, or about your purpose or intentions, or with your, perhaps intended, status or position. The danger signals are unrealistic time frames or motives, incompetence, or the total reliance upon circumstances or others. Possibly your actions or ambitions are more forceful than your character, abilities, or resources. This is the time to review your plans, and consolidate resources. The answer lies in you being more content in yourself first, and not so reliant upon others' attitude towards you, or in the (usually, future) situation to provide it all for you. Avoid the temptations of easy offers, long contracts, or risk. You need to find your own 'working level' now, and your own level of comfort.

You may be confident, and perhaps used to getting what you want, but here you face a situation, or a mishap, that stops you, or cautions you to wait. You may be under the impression that, whatever happens, you have enough resources to cope. Unfortunately there is more to life than your strength or resources. General circumstances, over which you have no control, sometimes mean that planning and strength cannot always be exercised, which will leave you somewhat at a loss. If you will be guided by prevailing conditions you can still achieve your aims, but not within the restrictive time limits you have set. Delay is a factor you must consider and account for in your plans. To ignore or overlook the possibility of delay in any human dealings is to chance failure.

The world is not such a bad place, but you have an inner dissatisfaction, or desire for more, which is causing the problems. With a little flexibility, and a little more time, you will find that the world will provide more, and take less. Recognise this, and have the relaxed confidence to walk away from, or around, the present issue or problem, not straight into it. Look where you are going.

ASSUMPTIONS OR RESOURCES

76
INDEPENDENT

You have abilities, skills, or an approach, that may not be recognised or understood at first, and which might prove awkward. There is here the feeling of being 'an outsider' and, in a mundane sense, this could find expression in sexual or spiritual minority groups, or be to do with your race or health, that makes you 'stand apart'. This may be obvious or  concealed. You can, and do, live with this. There will be 'social mobility', even adventure, because of your nature, talents, or periodic changes in identity and location.

In matters of attitude and inner motivation and satisfaction you are actually independent enough to make the most of the situation, but you may have to be devious or subtle, or maintain an outward appearance of conformity. Do not let this worry you. This is something that will always apply to you – find your own level within yourself first, then in society.

Your particular talent, lifestyle, interests, or activity, may need some active (self) promotion. This is a case, not of a lack of opportunity, but failing to make use of opportunities. You flourish when you take an unconventional route. You could re-define and re-present your work, or image, for 'mass consumption' or greater appeal, or go for the limited market. You will at some point be self-employed, work from home, or work 'unsocial hours', to suit yourself. Proceed as others in your field of activity, but be mobile, in finances and location, and continually adapt to the situation. Continuous output or activity will lead you to success and fulfilment.

You will have to cope with the fate of circumstances when you have to keep your inner-most heart a secret. However, when two people share the same path they have the power to change the world if they have a mind to. Your unconventional talent, approach, style, or 'individuality', is the way to success and happiness. You are in some way 'above average'. *Now flourish !*

CONFORM OR EXPLOIT

77

ASSERTION

 Someone, or some situation, makes demands on your time, your practicality, or good nature. There may be emotional, or dependency, complications with family or work. You need to learn to say "No", or, at least, make excuses, or keep your distance. This may require a tactical withdrawal. With the nature you have, you should always see to your own needs first, before you deal with others, otherwise you will resent your over-generous responses and 'self-less' acts. Always doing favours for others could be a sign of low self esteem, or a need to apologise for the incompetence of others. You'll need to be aware of how others use you. With your automatic response of generosity, it's time you realised that your own interests, fun and freedom, come first, and only then should you prioritise others.

Perhaps you need to take responsibility for your own life, interests, and comfort, and not blame circumstances or others. Just say what you want. There is no need to demand or apologise. If you wish to help, or to be of service to others, confine this to your professional life only. You can, of course, avoid or ignore this advice, and make any number of excuses for others, or your own good intentions, in a situation that seems to pay little regard for your well-being.

Because of your easy-going or caring nature, that doesn't want to offend, you comply with something that you should avoid or navigate around. However, there are times when firm action is required to remove an obstruction, or an apparently harmless request, or intrusion into your time. This may require a flat matter-of-fact refusal, with no emotion or apology, an abrupt withdrawal, or legal constraints. Take a detached view at what is going on and decide whether this, for someone else, is fair, proper, or considerate, and follow that conclusion yourself. In some cases the person, or situation, and its' influence, must be energetically stopped at once for your own future well-being and progress. If not, the situation will get worse, since the interference is intentional, or predictable. Be firm now, otherwise an overly considerate approach will be taken advantage of.

OBLIGATION   OR   FREEDOM

78
CONSOLIDATE

There may be some delays, obstructions, and perhaps even criticism of your actions or abilities. Always in such circumstances, stay calm and don't react. You do have a quiet inner strength that sees you through. In fact your natural strength of character allows you to maintain your position without having to demonstrate or prove yourself.

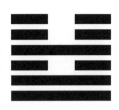

It is often in times of uncertainty that others push forward to take control, either by force, or distraction. You have the option to stand well back from the concerns and involvements of others. The source of the problem has its' own agenda and internal problems, indicated by the nature of the interference. If you are obliged to justify yourself, or forced to react, say or do nothing, or as little as possible.

You may, or may not, be in a strong position materially, but your inner peace comes from 'letting things be' without judgement, justification, or interference. A relaxed attitude, and a little enthusiasm, will not only answer, but improve, your situation. Leave it to events to unfold as they will, to your benefit.

This may now be the time to review your situation and long term plans, not in response to others but, as part of a quiet assessment of your future. You have potential, and a simple plan outline or list of requirements would reveal a lot, and provide a way forward. It is not more effort you need now, but a relaxed confidence.

CALM AND QUIET

81
AMBITION

 You are driven by material demands or the acquisition of status or security, which could become obsessive. There is an important distinction between the desire for immediate comforts, and the ambitions for a better lifestyle, status, power, and future rewards. Material circumstances may indeed offer you all you desire, or the prospects for it, but the price you pay is in your total commitment to the unending demand for more. Even so, you will achieve your ambitions, but the balance could be upset by opposition or envy.

Ambition can become an endless form of desire and gratification, and, ultimately a way of life. Ambition is, more often than not, a state of mind, rather than a convenient course of action. With ambition there is always the promise of reward, or the threat of competition, which, of course, provides the incentive. Such ambition is often satisfied, only to be replaced with further incentives. This route is self-perpetuating in the desire, not for rewards, but for more involvement and control. Here you appear to be in such a situation.

If you were to increase your efforts or control you would invite opposition. If you were to stop, you would, no doubt, feel empty, bored or loose your direction, and face a loss of identity or status. The way to succeed at this time is to keep a reasonable balance between status and involvement, and your own enjoyment in life. Your strength (and enjoyment or fulfilment) lies in your drive, not your status, or possessions. By all means pursue your natural talents and ambitions, but not at the expense of the influence you might have if you were to notice, and possibly help, others and the situation around you. If you must pursue 'one way', make sure it is a path that you could use again.

Go for variety, and share your interests and enjoyments. You have an abundance of energy. Control it wisely, otherwise it will defeat you, or divert you, one way or another. An increase in power or status does not automatically confer greater happiness or protection from unfortunate chance events, and your drive may be overtaken or diminished through personal problems. If you are clever or generous you could extend your influence further, towards popularity or fame. If you remain modest, even greater influence can be achieved.

OBSESSION   OR   ACQUISITION

82
PLEASURE

Fun, excitement, indulgence, or luxury, are on offer. There is some, perhaps lasting, fulfilment in your activities, your social life, or in your personal outlook. Maybe it's just time to congratulate yourself, or look forward to success. You can afford to be relaxed and confident, and you attract others and more good fortune. All of this suggests that you can get a  great deal of pleasure and material satisfaction from your particular circumstances, and you could seek more. It seems your pleasure is only limited by your enthusiasm and optimism.

'Perfection' may appear to be an impossible dream, unless you can find it in the ordinary everyday world. You could take this principle to mystical or spiritual lengths. Use your imagination, not just take what is offered.

INDULGENCE OR INVOLVEMENT

83
ENTHUSIASM

 You are enthusiastic, and it is your enthusiasm that people respond to. Enthusiasm comes from an inner impulse, regardless of conditions or circumstances. Outer conditions can, of course, dampen your enthusiasm, but providing you maintain your resolve and optimism, enthusiasm can, and will, change everything. Doubt, negativity, and reason, can kill enthusiasm, so go on your heart, not your head. It is time to do what you want to do, regardless of the reasons not to. Enthusiasm knows no bounds, and follows no reason or logic. Enthusiasm moves mountains, things, and people.

You are a 'creative dreamer', who might live 'in a world of your own', maybe for the whole of your life, or, at some point, 'get practical' and transform the world, for yourself and others. That opportunity is now with you. Artist or visionary, the danger is that you may be such 'a dreamer' as to not apply your powers for personal, material, or practical, gain. You should always use your enthusiasm to express what you know, or want.

It is your personal energy, as enthusiasm, that is directing events. Your enthusiasm can overcome any obstacle, and any task may be taken-on, no matter how difficult. You have access to the energy that is not worn-down by the world. Even though this may seem largely a matter of belief or trust, it does have the power to actually change material conditions, and influence people. Use your enthusiasm and adapt it to the needs of the situation, without rule, or condition. Apply it on every social and personal level at any time. With an open, enthusiastic, and friendly nature, you have the ability to enthuse and encourage others.

Your enthusiasm acts as a light to others. Your self confidence or inner nature attracts others, and you have the formula for success. 'By being relaxed and confident, and comfortable in yourself, the world follows you'. You will gain the support, friendship, and confidence, of others, so that you can achieve great things. You lead by example. *Inspire people !*

DREAMER OR TRANSFORMER

84
ORDER

The need for order arises when the world is full of diversity, variety, chance and change. Unfortunately, that order could represent conditioned responses, rigid and inflexible attitudes, a sense of duty or fixed identity, or being 'set in your ways'. Self-justification, oppression, and heavy responsibilities, are the danger signals. You do need a framework for action, or a plan,  but this does not necessarily mean strict control or a rigid structure. The more opportunities open to you, the more you may be inclined to overdo it. You can afford to be a bit more flexible and adaptable in your approach, based upon clear-cut objectives. You, of all people, have the ability to relax and thrive in any ordered situation, and gain more strength from it.

You have an aptitude for facts or figures, and an attention to detail. Your 'routine', method, or way of working, may rely on concentrated effort, so you should be careful of obsession or exhaustion. Do not allow your capacity to organise things become greater than your natural drive and enthusiasm. Even in an ordered life there is room for spontaneity. This is really about the wise (and ease of) management of human, personal, and material resources. Order cannot be demanded, or controlled by effort, without disruptive opposition. Accept the situation for whatever it is, for you have the time and energy to achieve a great deal if you are guided by your own interest and enthusiasm.

If you cannot share your enthusiasm, either proceed alone, or be a lot more subtle in your approach.

OPPORTUNITY   OR   OPPRESSION

85
DURATION

You are entering into a long phase, relationship, or undertaking, and a period of social and material fulfilment. You can respond to this with an active involvement, or with a relaxed confidence by letting events decide what you do. To persist over a long period requires patience and adaptability. There may well be a number of personal and social changes, but do not confuse changing times and the diversity of worldly, social, and personal events, with your inner nature which remains the same. Even though gain and loss are inevitable, the longer you are in the game, the stronger you get. For you it is a matter of maintaining an inner sense of proportion that will give you the benefits of duration – understanding, acceptance, and optimism.

Duration does not imply a long static situation. On the contrary, there is movement and change all the time, so that a fixed attitude will quickly be overtaken by events. Maintain a balance between planned progress and spontaneous expression, and always make allowances for the timing of events, by factoring-in the possibility of delay.

Change will provide you with all the chances for development you need, and also provide a 'freshness' to events. There will always be something to grab your attention, to get you involved, or cause you to react. If you can see all of this involvement in an 'overall sense' with a little detachment, you will know when to adapt, and when to stand well back. "Pace yourself" – it's the way of coping with change.

You could, when, and if, you are ready, move from an 'active, ongoing, productive life' to a state of harmony, detachment, and inner peace. The more you relax, the further you go.

PACE OR RACE

86
INTEGRATE

When you are ready, there are new responsibilities and rewards awaiting you. You are able to integrate into many areas, some of which may not be entirely sympathetic to your cause, because it is people you influence, not systems. Proceed in an apparently harmless way in order to gain your objectives. It is by breaking down the barriers between people, not holding  views or territory, that you extend your influence, communicate, and promote. To do this you must pose no threat, listen (be interested), and show enthusiasm for some cause or outlook, while at the same time not expecting any response, recognition, or reward, for your standpoint or endeavours. Be subtle, use humour, and your ability to get on with others.

Have an open mind and adapt your plans as you go along. There is a distinct possibility that you will gain a reputation, and that you, or your work, will gain the attention of a great number of people. A cohesive plan here, or distant travel, could have a successful outcome. Develop your powers of explanation and expression. This is the time for self-promotion and wider communication in order to extend your influence over a much wider area. Think worldly !

RECOGNITION   OR   REPUTATION

87
INCREASE

There is an increase in your status or possessions. There may be more enthusiasm or activity, and good health. Progress is indicated through changing circumstances. There is good fortune from your particular involvements and connections. If this increase in activity and reward is have any real benefit it should be directed by a plan. Your enthusiasm and motivation will now bring about what you desire. Go for it with confidence. This is a time when you make progressive steps towards self-fulfilment. Take every option now.

INTEREST   OR   INVESTMENT

88

EXCESS

More indulgence or greater consumption will lead to problems. Unless you are very careful the consequences could be addiction, over-discipline, exhaustion, or collapse. There is too much involvement present, in greed (wilful energy), or too little, in the form of boredom (uncontrolled energy). There is a lack of personal fulfilment, and you try to fill the gap with  consumption, or struggle, as the answer, and merely divert the same energy elsewhere. Satisfying yourself in diversionary activities is a way to compensate for unfortunate events or upsets, but you are over doing it !

Trying to solve your problems with obsessive control, or indulgence, only adds to your problems. It is not compensation you need, but an improvement in existing conditions or aspirations, then you will find a natural way to happiness and approval. If you let your present position, possessions, or desires, dictate your actions, you can expect misfortune. To cling on to your previous way or objectives would be a mistake. You have the required strength and intelligence to avoid approaching disaster, but only if you act wisely (an aspect not shown so far).

You are warned that the excess shown here, in your reactions, ambition, involvement, or consumption, can have dramatic consequences if not tackled. You must retreat or give-up some ground. This will be awkward for you. Material things can be replaced, and you have the energy to do this, but emotional responses take more time to sort-out. This, however, looks unlikely because of your strong desire to indulge or escape. The first step is to acknowledge the facts, then to have a wish to change things. At this stage do not even consider the 'how', 'when', or 'where'. You don't need force or strong action only a transition phase, or 'cooling off' period, to give yourself some time to reassess and think about, not all the problems, but the improvements.

If things are 'all wrong', they need to be 'all right', and to be 'alright' in yourself is the first step. This is an inner mental state, not induced by drugs, indulgence, or lifestyle, which you'll find in the space between what you are doing now, and what you would like to be doing. For most people this space is filled with hope, ambition, nostalgia and justification [usually thoughts and plans], but you have filled it with your present activities [indulgence or control]. The 'space' is the 'inner' space you inhabit right now, but you are probably unaware of it because you can only see, and feel, what you have filled it with. For you, this inner space (in some sense, your mind) needs to be empty ! With all your previous activity and worry this will sound odd, and probably out of the question.

Live for, and in, the present, for no reason at all, not even for pleasure or disappointment ! You'll need to be awake and alert to do this, for the rewards and effects are both subtle and informative. Your situation will provide the simple comforts (use them), and the people to guide you (as well as the HEXAGRAMS). You are NOT going anywhere, so avoid obvious temptations and distractions. Don't worry, you won't escape pleasure or disappointment, they are automatic. Just stay as alert and as comfortable as you can, in the present. Don't think about the future, or the past. Maybe, don't think. Your mind needs to be clear and calm.

Of course, you may argue that it is the present that you are trying to avoid, but actually this isn't the case. The present is empty and benign (that is, friendly), apart from all your thoughts, reactions, and responses that you have added in. The world neither knows nor cares what you do, so it's up to you how you cope with this. There is love, comfort, duty, involvement, and all the rest of it on offer. Let TAO show you what's on offer. You certainly don't want to miss some very subtle offers, big surprises, and, *"when the energy flows, – interesting times"*. The how, when, and where, is now handled by TAO. Just observe the strange ways of the world.

With that 'empty' mind, 'just living in the present', you are now told something you would, possibly, never accept or know. You will always draw a full life to yourself. Enjoy this attraction you have, but don't you get *so caught up* in all the involvements and desires. "Relax Dude !"

PLENTY   OR   EXHAUSTION

THE MYSTIC LIFE

Steps To Take You Beyond

The mystic life is a full integration with the everyday world around you as it is now. It is not a matter of being good, or striving to make the world a more spiritual place, or seeking answers or teachers, or waiting for some future state. **It is here, now, flowing through you.**

The flow of energy is automatic and has very little to do with you. As an agent of TAO you are not here to serve it, change it, or improve it, but simply be yourself. What TAO wants from you will be presented to you each week, and you will promote either more Inflowing Energy or more Outflowing Energy by your thoughts and actions. You are nothing but the spiritual manifestation and materialisation of the energy that flows through you. You are the gateway through which the energy flows. Two thousand years ago a Taoist monk was given Enlightenment with the proposition

"Everyone follows the true path. Can you see it ?"

This is 'the Way in Humans', and it can be seen as a flow of energy. The modern day mystic is aware of the intangible forces at play in the world, and lives a 'spiritual life' in a material world. To live a spiritual life is to extend your influence in the world, to others, for no other reason than it makes you smile (as you will find out). Such activity increases energy. This is done by simply observing without immediately reacting, judging, or justifying. You need to be aware of that profound blend of situation, timelessness, and place. In some sense nothing is going on, except you !, and yet anything is possible. To you, here, now, there is a magical 'offering' and perpetual 'availability' through flowing energy.

The mystic life is living in the real world as you let Outflowing Energy flow out through you, without your intervention or interference. Being 'spiritual' is positively and lightly influencing others, and your environment, without ulterior motives, and with no thought of reward. This is sometimes called 'unconditional love', but is so often confused and conditioned by notions of good and bad, sacrifice and altruism.

A DUTY

TO SAVE

US ALL

You cannot force, ask, or invite, without the reaction of Inflowing Energy. You cannot stop Inflowing Energy, and you cannot influence it. In much the same way, chance and change happen to all! Chance and change rule the material world, not effort and control, so that all you can do is be receptive enough to observe and adapt, as you go along.

Everyone has a choice. You can choose involvement and concern, that appears full and offers results and rewards, or choose an easy approach, which is so spontaneous that contentment seems elusive. Most, reasonably, take the first choice and never realise or notice the implications. Concerned involvement – Inflowing Energy – is the status quo. This is it! What you've got now is your lot, and for some it is imperative that they maintain this. The attraction is that it could be pleasurable, profitable, or powerful, and promises more, but this is as far as it goes. *Endlessly involved in itself.*

Outflowing Energy is a movement of energy that extends and shows more of what is. All of this requires a fundamental shift in your awareness or attention. Look out, not in to your own thoughts and notions. They will remain, but not to dominate and control your life. Look around you, and leave the rest to TAO.

Initially you may not see this flow of energy, but the effects will never cease to amuse, delight, amaze, and surprise, you ! Actually the first indication you have may be a feeling of 'lightness' or quietness, or a hint of enthusiasm. You will come to relish identifying and meeting Inflowing Energy in whatever form it takes. Sometimes you step to one side, and sometimes you get the opportunity to use Outflowing Energy. Give people time, recognize them, and listen. Pass on optimism, encouragement, and enthusiasm, *regardless of the circumstances*, or just smile. When you smile you convert energy. You share Outflowing Energy without even thinking about it. Lighten every room you enter. You conduct the flow of your energy through others, things, and places. This is what TAO does all the time.

THE ENERGY FLOW IN YOUR LIFE

Inflowing Energy	Outflowing Energy
▬▬▬▬▬	▬▬ ▬▬
FIXED STANDARDS	FLUID SIMPLICITY
justification & judgement	observation & acceptance
REACTION CONVENTION	QUIET UNDERSTANDING
comparison	compassion
seeking & striving	seeing & letting go
TAKE	**GIVE**
possession & investment	impersonal giving
" IT'S NOT EASY "	" IT IS ! "

That's all you can do is give out all the time, for you do not hold on to energy, thoughts, or attitudes. You give out what others cannot see, or don't want, even though they are pre-disposed, with the energy they have, to 'take all they can'. *You share something vast !*

TAO

147

"Going With The Flow"

*How to let go of Inflowing Energy
and let Outflowing Energy flow through you.*

" GIVE UP "
looking elsewhere

There is no book, system, philosophy, or belief, that will change your attitude, but merely reflect what you already know to be true.

THE FOUNDATION
OF KNOWLEDGE

A 3000 year old Chinese manuscript, that contains the Meaning of Life, was painstakingly translated into Greek, and hand copied onto vellum by monks in a Southern Italian monastery around 900 A.D. The text was revised between 1610 – 1860, and today there seems to be some dispute over the authorized interpretation.

You will never give-up the desire for more information, more excitement and novelty, or more recognition, but you can

just stop for a moment, and

" GIVE IN "
to all the notions

that you could change anything. Let your brain think what it wants because it simply repeats Inflowing Energy. You worry and think too much. You'll always be facing new problems and emotions because there is no end to what the world, and others, can throw at you. Your thoughts and reactions will never leave you alone.

Accept this is how it is, and

" GIVE OUT "
without fear

Relax that material and mental hold. You won't loose it all, and if you were going to be taken advantage of, it's probably already too late. Be open. Always be ready to give, when asked. What you give out, you get back, increased. That's the way energy is.

148

To those caught-up in the flow of Inflowing Energy, the prospect of release is either nonsensical or elusive. You can't try, or practice, or use a method, to change your energy flow, for that simply reinforces Inflowing Energy. Discursive thoughts about anything and everything will occupy your mind most of the time, as well as justifications, ambitions, desires, and identity. Emotions, experiences, and memories, as well as logic and reason, also condition not only what you think, but how you think. You are well and truly caught, but you'll call it 'life', although it may be more like a very involved, emotional, and self-centred, dream. *Whatever your status or position in life, you will not be free of the influence of Inflowing Energy* until you can look at the one choice. Reaction or relaxation. *You decide, moment by moment, what measure* of either *you want.*

'Nothing is going on', except you. If you think there is, you will be endlessly involved in all the powerful arguments, theories, and reasons, and their consequences. There may in fact be a lot going on, and anything can happen, and Inflowing Energy will keep you involved to the exclusion of everything else. There is no completion, no limited time, *only your involvement.* Whatever you decide to think and do, everything develops and changes, and sometimes into its' opposite. You can see this if you care to look, and notice a whole different flow of energy that hasn't really got anything to do with you. This strange awareness is heartening, quiet, and often liberating. All of this does not mean that you can not achieve anything, or should not plan and progress, but only accept that most things are not final or complete and are always open to change and chance. This is another way of saying, just look at the flow of the present moment.

The issue, or perceived threat here, is to your own self identity, direction, and intentions. It is the absolute need to have an opinion, attitude, status or identity, work or family, to support your life, to give you direction, meaning, or recognition. You need all of this to express yourself, to feel useful, powerful, or loved. Unfortunately, this involvement can, but need not, obscure everything else. You can be who you want, *and* see the present moment, as it continually changes. TAO, this present moment, not only sustains you, but offers endless opportunities, sights and wonders, through chance and change. You can do whatever you want, but use Outflowing Energy, which has an increasing potential, and will cause other subtle shifts in your own state of happiness and well-being. The solution is to 'not think', and simply look at, and listen to, the world, and relate to others, through an attentive awareness or sensitivity. You can 'activate' this *only in the present*, here now. This is the enlightenment and huge liberation.

It's time for you to live in the present.

149

The Mystic Gateways

Your personal and social world thrives on Inflowing Energy, and yet the Natural World, the environment, the elements and weather and sky, and the spaces around you, are full of Outflowing Energy. You can 'tune-in' to this energy. The HEXAGRAMS of The TAO I CHING provide an easy introduction to this energy, but there are other Mystic Gateways. You 'activate' or physically pass through a Mystic Gateway by simply looking and listening. This is essentially a subtle shift in your awareness. The 'spontaneous and flexible system' to see and use TAO, could be YOU, through a number of Mystic Gateways.

The modern day mystic lives in this world with inner peace, spontaneity, intuition, and the guidance of the qualities of light, sound, movement, and space, through the act of sharing. You do this 'sharing', by simply 'pouring out' your attention or interest onto something. Here, it is very much like the notion of 'unconditional love', which you direct, unseen by others, with no thought other than to share. That sharing is not taken from the outside world, but flows out from your own heart. This is not about helping others, or the planet, or even being compassionate. You simply share your heart (sensitivity or feelings) with something else, which could be an animal, plant, object, a possession, a person, or any thing around you, through observation.

By giving your complete attention you become open enough to communicate with all things, and you will find that *all things are alive*. You could start 'outpouring' for five minutes a day. Pick any living thing (to start with), - an animal, plant or tree, for instance [but not a person]. You would have to exercise some caution when dealing with people because of the intimate energies used, and their effects, and such an approach may be more suited to therapy or healing work, or to your emotional life. You can also do this with inanimate objects (furniture, objects, stones), enclosed spaces (rooms, gardens), and, when you are ready, open spaces (parks, streets, sky, night time).

By being completely open with something, you share, and what you give out is returned in a different form. Usually this is in the form of 'sensual or sensitive' feelings, or 'information' which can be translated into words or concepts. Of course, when dealing with Nature or the elements, those 'concepts' may be quite unfamiliar, with some difficulty in expressing them in words. Trees, especially at night, will talk to you if you listen, but it can be a strange communication. Apart from any 'information' you receive, what you'll find is that the more you share, the more 'joy', acceptance, peace of mind, strength and comfort, *will be added to you*. It is poured in from above, into the top of your head, and you are filled with lightness. In your daily life you will notice the difference. If you continue to 'pour out', you become 'overflowing', and "Shine Out". It is this quality that can be seen (by a few others, and) in others, and in things, as a sense of presence *in all things*.

Here is an easy introduction to what surrounds you *all the time.*

The Quality of Light

Just observe the changing light through the day, and through the Seasons. You are not looking at anything in particular, although each thing is changed by the light. Look at 'the feeling' of the daylight, or the light cast by lamp or fire. This act of looking allows Outflowing Energy to flow better. The light itself has a quality to it that is 'diffused', or 'full', or 'sharp' and revealing, etc. The light shows, and changes, the world around you, and supports you when you need it. It is this light, at dawn or dusk, the play of sunlight, or on overcast days, that hints at a 'comforting condition'. Even a few minutes a day silently observing the quality of light will have a deep calming effect on your life, which you will notice in a week.

The quality of light is part of a more encompassing state, in which, in each place or space, there is a different 'atmosphere', or feeling, beyond the obvious. You could notice this difference when you are in your car, and then step-out onto the street, or when you enter a large shop, an office, or room. Each place or space has the accumulated energy of what fills it, as well as the light. Be a little more receptive to the feeling of that space, rather than its' obvious function or use, because that 'atmosphere' affects you and others. You may not be able to change the atmosphere of a place, (you may not get the chance to shine-up anything) but you can determine its' underlying 'resonance' or energy beyond the activity in it. Meanwhile, in each place and time, just look at, and appreciate, the quality of light. It is this awareness that leads to the insight that there is a lot more going on that you may have failed to notice. It is through this Gateway that you step into TAO. *Welcome !*

Energy Moves

Look at the movement around you. The sky and weather are good places to start, to appreciate that this movement is in four dimensions (or more), and not strictly going to, or in, one place. Movement surrounds you all the time, both physically and mentally. If you live in the city, all that traffic and rush appears to be going somewhere, but is only an expression of concentrated energy. Each movement, in Nature or Man, promotes either Inflowing Energy or Outflowing Energy. You decide which. Start with river water, and notice how many different states and changes there are. The current may be fast and 'urgent', or slow and meandering in a 'lazy' flow, or perhaps still, deep, and 'quiet'. In the behaviour of people around you, look at the 'speed' of the energy flow, and notice the consequences. Look at people in public, and see if you can identify the degree of tension, force, or control, from their movements, even when they sit in a café, or on a train. In human society most of this is on an inner emotional (Inflowing Energy) level of involvement and concern. You might be able to sense the direction of the flow of that energy.

Here the TRIGRAMS come in useful in identifying the direction of the flow of energy. By putting a number (1-8) to the main effect of the energy you have a short-hand method of assessment. Each TRIGRAM represents a 'speed' and a direction when applied to situations, events, and even people (and when you have a HEXAGRAM you can also translate the TRIGRAMS to energy flow). This is part of 'seeing the world symbolically' in energy terms. After a little familiarization, you will associate the state' or 'the movement' simply by using the TRIGRAM numbers of this Energy Formula.

THE ENERGY FORMULA WITH TRIGRAM NUMBERS

active - fast	**1**	PUSH	Inflowing Energy
flowing – easy	**2**	LET GO	Outflowing Energy
increasing - fast	**3**	OPEN	Outflowing Energy
fixed – static	**4**	HOLD	Inflowing Energy
falling – stop/start	**5**	BEND	Inflowing Energy
flat – busy	**6**	PULL	Inflowing or Outflowing Energy
rising - slow	**7**	PRESS	Inflowing or Outflowing Energy
decreasing – slow	**8**	USE	Inflowing or Outflowing Energy

It is through movement that energy finds expression. By being open, you can go with ease, and 'go with the flow'. By being still 'within', you let the energies flow unrestricted. Through this stillness, at the centre of all the movement of the world, is your Gateway.

Beyond the movement around you, you also go at a 'speed', not only physically, but mentally in your thoughts and concerns. There is no need for all this extra movement unless you want to produce more Inflowing Energy to support your lifestyle or ambitions. It is the involved thoughts, plans, and expectations, that keep your mind moving, perhaps, faster than your physical body.

You will use your body and your mind to encourage, or compensate for, this 'speed' of life. All of this requires a great amount of energy, which you may be unaware that you were using, or you may indeed be aware of the effects of stress. To slow the movement down you need to put your attention on 'the outside', what is around you *now*, not 'the inside', what you think and worry about (in the past or in the future). Those involved thoughts will not leave you alone unless you change the direction of the flow of energy going through you.

To change the direction, 'look out, not inwards.' At any time you can stop speculating for a moment, and give your mind something else to do. There are sights, sounds, and sensations, around you all the time. You pay no attention to these because they apparently serve no useful purpose. If pleasure or pain was involved they would have your complete attention ! These subtle, present, moving, and changing, sights and sounds *are there to inform, amuse, and guide you*. There is in all of this a gentle 'flow' of energy, but you have to slow-down enough to perceive it. That 'slowing-down' isn't going slower, it is going in another direction, which, from the position and speed of Inflowing Energy, can appear slower, stopped, or even going 'backwards'. Energy always moves. It never stops or 'subtracts'. The rush of Inflowing Energy doesn't get you to the present moment any faster. You are already here.

The Energy Formula highlights an unexpected point. A closer look at the formula will show that OPEN energy **3** (LOOK), providing vitality and enthusiasm, is as fast and powerful as PUSH (GO) energy **1**. The energy from looking and being open is not as passive in energy terms as it usually appears to be.

The Sound of Silence

Listen for the sound of silence. You won't hear it, but what you do hear is the sound of the world around you. This can be soft and far away, or noisy, or 'perpetual', and in all of this 'something is going on' without your involvement or noise. Listen to the sounds you personally make or cause. Each sound alters the atmosphere *and connects you and things to the physical and material world*, through anything from traffic noise to birdsong. Listen for unexpected sounds that draw, or shock, you back into the 'reality' of the world, or for 'inappropriate', or surprising sounds that alert you to the humour and nonsense of it all.

Sound is bound-up with movement, and reflects precisely the level of Inflowing Energy present. In music, for instance, you could identify the 'emotional movement' of rising and falling energy. The number one hit pop songs and ballads will use the Energy Formula of STOP/START/FALLING energy **5** and HOLD energy **4**, because they deny or delay, then promise more (Inflowing Energy and involvement) to hold on to. Classical music will have the full range, and your choice reflects what you need to satisfy your energy needs.

Meanwhile, apart from the comforting or important sounds of the world, only within you is a profound silence. You won't be aware of this except perhaps in meditation. You don't need to listen for this silence, but instead listen to the world with its' noise, sounds, music, and chatter, but from a quiet centre. Now you will start to sense that other inner dimension from which you operate, through simple observation. Come out into the world full of noise and bustle where TAO flows in all directions. What you'll find is that the quieter you go through the world, the more it sings to you. Through this Gateway you enter TAO.

Timeless Space

The space around you now is a Gateway to another very subtle dimension, and unless you are still and quiet you will miss it entirely. This other dimension is a sensibility or awareness that you occupy, **not** a place (that you identify) or time (whatever day it is, or, indeed, however old you might be). The space around you is timeless, and if you 'stop' you can live in it. [Trees inhabit this same timeless space].

Meanwhile, others can be distracted by the noise and diversions, and 'wander off' into the scene, or into their mind. If you look at a picture or photograph you tend to completely ignore the fact that it is only a flat piece of paper, while you enter into its' world. Here is the same sensation, where you choose to ignore an 'obvious' spiritual dimension so that you can 'step into', and be involved in, the world. This, here and now, is so easy to attain, and yet it is unknown or unobserved because it is 'on the surface' or 'close to', while your attention is drawn into the involvements of the world.

The first step is to think of your present surroundings as a *space, not a place*, as though it were completely alien to you. The second step is to quietly look around you *without any thoughts* or preferences, *as an observer only*, and you will notice that *time stands still*, even though things and people move about. When you first do this, maybe with others around you, or other things going on, you will get a sensation of this timelessness. This is your first glimpse, for it develops into a more profound awareness that makes a huge impact on your life.

You can gain access to this sensation or quiet at any time. How strange that the world and everything in it moves, and your body moves, and yet you look-on from a still centre. [You can see how trees are disposed to this state]. This timeless centre is TAO, and you have accessed it, and are it. You have found the discovery made thousands of years ago by the ancient Chinese. You possess the same qualities as TAO, and this quiet strength and awareness allows you to operate in the world with inner peace, enjoyment, and spontaneity. Through this Gateway you enter the spiritual life.

Through these Mystic Gateways you enter the world of Chance and Change. TAO *is the visible working of Outflowing Energy in the world, through chance and change.* These changes can only happen in a situation that is built for this very purpose – *the present* – and this is where you observe them, or deal with them.

The Mechanics of TAO

TAO exists to provide whatever material conditions, emotional activity, or spiritual comfort, you need, regardless of who you are. TAO *unfolds, most strange of all, at your pace, and to your limits.* You can see TAO working in 'one off' events that appear randomly, or happen automatically, without, as it were, human control. These 'events' are the gateways to awareness.

These are basically a wake-up call to alert your attention to the movement of energy, of which you are a part. From these events you will see the way TAO operates through you, if you let it, by stopping, helping, repeating, responding, giving, and reflecting. However, to those that use Inflowing Energy all of these events act as a trigger for more reaction and further involvement.

COINCIDENCE   *Parallel events.*

Your words or thoughts are repeated simultaneously by others, in overheard conversation, or in the media. Alternatively, your actions or intentions are carried out at the same time by someone else, and you can view the consequences. The actual words or actions are not important here, only the simultaneous repetition.

PROVE IT FOR YOURSELF

Make a note of coincidences, or similarities, not just dismiss them because they seem disconnected or serve no apparent purpose. This attention leads to a greater awareness of how things are connected, and also how 'impersonal' it all is.

INCIDENCE   *Directional events.*

An overlapping event that interrupts and momentarily stops your words or actions. There may be delays or postponements, or repeated mishaps that caution you to wait, or you may be stopped from doing or saying something. Heed the warning, although you can override the circumstances. These INCIDENCES can be ignored, but you would have to 'repeat yourself' to complete the task. They are, however, invariably for your benefit or information.

PROVE IT FOR YOURSELF

Slow down a bit and listen when you are talking, and observe your own over-riding impulses.   Watch-out for INCIDENCES in the form of spontaneous overlapping actions, which happen frequently, to alter an intended direction (for yourself, or others).

INTERVENTION   *Control events.*

These are the chance events that actually stop you, and change your, possibly planned, routine or course. This will involve the timing, or being at the wrong place at a certain time. Even though diverted by cancellation, delay, misfortune, accident, or personal mistake, the new situation presented will reward you, with new options, or redress the balance and compensate you for any loss. When there is a significant delay, or cancellation, in your plans, look again at what you ultimately gain or learn. Reaction here will only involve you further. When INTERVENTIONS happen, do not react, remain receptive, and *the situation itself* will adjust to protect, reward, or help you.

PROVE IT FOR YOURSELF

The next time you are held-up and are late for an appointment, notice the way the world will cover-up for you, or provide excuse or readjustment for your benefit.

REFLECTION   *Reflected events.*

If you are aware of something – an idea, a situation, event, or perhaps a new word – it is brought to your attention again automatically. An idea or notion that you have been thinking about may be expressed in a book that you pick up, or be explained to you, or someone you have been thinking about turns-up. You draw to yourself what you know to be true, or consider important, or catches your attention.

PROVE IT FOR YOURSELF

Pick any new word out of the dictionary *that appeals to you,* and wait for it to turn-up in conversation, or in the world.

RECEPTION   *Reciprocal events.*

What you give out you get back. This works materially, and through your attitude. Often when you seek to gain, at someone elses' expense, it is balanced by a subsequent loss. When you give spontaneously, as required by the situation, or without thought of reward, you will be rewarded in increased proportion.

PROVE IT FOR YOURSELF

The next time you are asked to give to charity, or to anyone, give spontaneously and generously, regardless of the rightness of the request. Make a note of your 'donation', and the increased return you receive later.

RESPONSE   *Attitude.*

As you approach the world, so you are treated. What you ask for, you get, but unfortunately not always as you expect. It is your intention (and the manner in which you ask) that is translated and returned to you in different forms, in material things, events, and situations. You may see your desires, or dissatisfaction, in the media, or even in someone else's life or possession. In short, your ATTITUDE IS REFLECTED. It is your attitude, not the 'thing' itself, that causes a response and reaction.

PROVE IT FOR YOURSELF

To demonstrate this, take a few moments to ask for a specific 'materialistic' item you desire – a yacht, large house, car, or large sum of money, perhaps. Do this with desire and wishful intention. (This would be the expression of Inflowing Energy). Now, wait for your desires to be reflected, or returned, to you through your letterbox.

PROVIDE   *The Timing.*

When timing is involved in any 'deal', change, or movement, that you require, it can *only* be provided by TAO. Accept this, and you will "go with the flow", and actually receive what you want at the right time. Whatever energy you use on worrying about the timing of events is counter-productive. Do all you are able to do, and allow things to happen spontaneously or a lot quicker, or slower, than you normally allow for. Leave the timing to TAO. This 'state of TRUST' has enormous energy and vitality implications.

PROVE IT FOR YOURSELF

All your deadlines will be met if you leave them entirely to TAO. Strangely enough, everything has a way of 'working out'.

AFFINITY   *Synchronicity.*

Your situation, problem, or progress, can be seen in other mechanical, scientific, or intuitive, systems. Your situation, question, or enquiry, can be answered, 'tied-into', presented or manifested in, another set of *totally unrelated options*. Obviously such systems as the Tarot, the Runes, or Astrology, will provide you with personal direction, information, and understanding, unavailable elsewhere, since they are designed to do so. However, ANY unrelated system could provide you with the insight, order, or the information you want. In a wider sense TAO also provides what you need, when you need it, and often in unexpected and 'unrelated' circumstances.

   PROVE IT FOR YOURSELF

Select a HEXAGRAM now, in response to a personal question.

"Inflowing Energy and Outflowing Energy change all conditions under Heaven.
In this great flow of energy Chance and Change dominate.
But above these, the present moment consumes everything.
And yet TAO contains all things.
TAO has no consciousness, no action, no intention.
It is the still centre of all movement and change.
Through Inflowing Energy and Outflowing Energy you enter TAO.
Choose rightly, for you change the entire universe by your Awareness."

                                                         WANG PI   246 A.D.

THE TAO I CHING

This version of the ancient Chinese classic "I Ching" goes back to the original insight of King Wēn (1231 – 1135 B.C.) with the main emphasis on two aspects of energy which predate the concepts of Yin and Yang, which were introduced into the text eight hundred years later. The commentary and sequence is by Wang Pi (226 – 249 A.D.). The numbering and text to the HEXAGRAMS will differ from other versions of The I Ching because the structure of the HEXAGRAM relates to two TRIGRAMS, and not the usual, often contradictory, four, with the meanings of the third and fourth TRIGRAMS reversed. The TAO I CHING is a stand-alone version that will give you a more in-depth, plain English, interpretation of your own energy, with practical advice and guidance for any situation. The TAO I CHING was designed to be used with a special set of ELEMENTS © to give you instant access to the HEXAGRAMS.

THE ELEMENTS ©

Provide easy instant access to all the HEXAGRAMS and changes,
in the TAO I CHING,
and for any edition of The I Ching.

www.taoiching.com

The Author

Tom Leworthy is an artist and writer, and professional TAO I CHING consultant. He has researched and written books on The I Ching, The Bhagavad Gita, and The New Testament Gospels, and produced a 12 Lesson Correspondence Course on Metaphysical Philosophy. He has had a number of spontaneous 'out of the body' experiences, as well as lucid dreaming. The concept of Mystic Gateways developed out of these experiences.

For a couple of years he produced and printed an alternative free magazine "Sparkly Light", distributed throughout Ceredigion and West Wales. More recently he has worked as a professional psychic clairvoyant.

www.taoiching.com

The traditional Three Coin Method to select the HEXAGRAM

If you do not possess a set of ELEMENTS © to access any of the HEXAGRAMS you will need to use the Three Coin Method. For this you will need three similar coins and a pen and paper. You can use any three similar denomination coins for this purpose. You could use Chinese coins, or mint British 2p coins (and used only for this purpose) are an excellent alternative.

For each question or enquiry you must cast, or throw, the three coins for each of the six lines of the HEXAGRAM, starting with the bottom line. Cup the three coins in both hands, shake them while you think of your question, and cast them onto a table. On the five subsequent throws of your three coins you build-up the HEXAGRAM, with the sixth throw as line 6 at the top.

Each time you cast the coins, make a note of the line it forms. Heads count as a whole line, and Tails as a divided line. Out of the three coins select the odd one out, to represent that line. Three Heads will be a whole line (which will change), and three Tails will be a divided line (which will similarly change). These are called Changing Lines. After you have consulted your HEXAGRAM, change any and all Changing Lines to their opposite, in one go. Through Changing Lines a second HEXAGRAM is formed.

FOR EACH THROW OF THE COINS

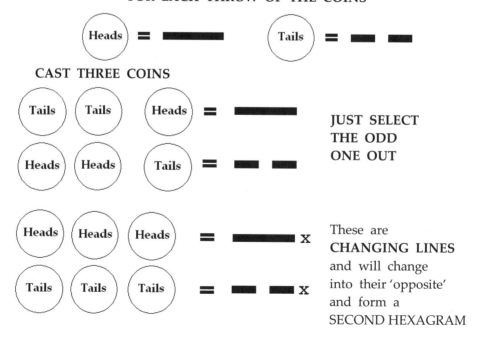

When a line is the result of three Heads or three Tails it is a CHANGING LINE, and marked with a little cross. These Changing Lines will change to their opposite to form a second HEXAGRAM. After consulting the first HEXAGRAM, *all* the Changing Lines are changed, *in one go*, to form the SECOND HEXAGRAM.

Example

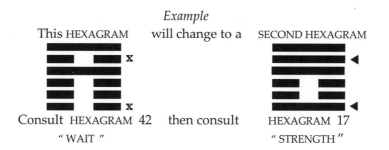

This HEXAGRAM   will change to a   SECOND HEXAGRAM

Consult HEXAGRAM 42   then consult   HEXAGRAM 17

" WAIT "   " STRENGTH "

This second HEXAGRAM represents the future development of the situation, or the resolution, or result, of your enquiry.

As you can see in the example above, the first HEXAGRAM may initially indicate a situation to which you could immediately react. Read the HEXAGRAM, for the situation and events may be trying to tell you something else, and the second HEXAGRAM may well indicate an insight, or the next step.